Twenty Years of Economic Reconstruction
in East Germany

Applied Economics Quarterly
Supplement

Issue 60

Twenty Years of Economic Reconstruction in East Germany

Edited by

Christian Wey
and Klaus F. Zimmermann

Duncker & Humblot · Berlin

Bibliographic information published by Die Deutsche Bibliothek

Die Deutsche Bibliothek lists this publication in the Deutsche Nationalbibliografie; detailed bibliographic data is available in the Internet at <http://dnb.ddb.de>.

Technical editor: Deborah Anne Bowen

Typesetting and printing:
Berliner Buchdruckerei Union GmbH, Berlin
Printed in Germany

ISSN 1612-2127
ISBN 978-3-428-13257-7

Printed on no aging resistant (non-acid) paper
according to ISO 9706 ♾

Internet: http://www.duncker-humblot.de

Editorial

This supplement to Applied Economics Quarterly reports on the 72nd Annual Meeting of the Association of German Economic Research Institutes (ARGE-Institute), which took place in Berlin on April 23, 2009. The topic was

"Twenty Years of Economic Reconstruction in East Germany."

This year, we celebrate the twentieth anniversary of German reunification. In February 1990, when political leaders proposed that the Deutsche Mark be introduced as the legal currency in the GDR, this idea was rejected unanimously by leading economic scholars. With the creation of the economic and currency union, a process of dynamic growth and development was launched in many areas of society. Looking back over these past two decades, the conference addressed two overarching questions: Where do we stand today, and what are the prospects for the future? What economic policy strategies are conceivable, and what needs to be undertaken politically to set the course?

The lectures focused on the following aspects: regional development and old-age poverty in East Germany, the returns to education among full-time employees in Germany, and the demand for skilled labor in Thuringia up to 2015.

We thank the federal government, particularly the Federal Ministry of Economics and Technology, for their generous support in making the conference possible.

We would like to thank Karl Brenke (DIW Berlin) for the conceptual preparation of the conference, the organizers, Susanne Marcus and Ralf Messer (ARGE-Institute), and all the participants and attendees for their contributions.

Next year's annual meeting will take place in April 2010 in Berlin and will address the theme "After the Crisis is before the Crisis".

June 2009

Christian Wey
Klaus F. Zimmermann

Contents

Twenty Years after the Fall of the Berlin Wall: Structural Convergence in a Slow-Growth Environment

By Markus Demary* and Klaus-Heiner Röhl**

Abstract

In this paper, we take a closer look at the development of the East German economy since German reunification in 1990 and its sectoral structure. Manufacturing has regained importance, driven by strong growth. Particularly in the southern East German states – Saxony, Saxony-Anhalt and Thuringia – manufacturing has grown rapidly and new industrial clusters have emerged. These states have experienced a substantially higher rate of growth in GDP per capita than the northern states Brandenburg, Mecklenburg-Western Pomerania and Berlin over the last eight years. In connection with the growth of manufacturing, the contribution of the joint federal-state regional investment incentives to the industrial build-up in East German regions will be examined using panel regressions. For this we apply a comprehensive dataset on investment incentives by region. The results show that investment incentives contribute substantially to regional growth in manufacturing. Moreover, we found significant employment effects for seventeen manufacturing industries and business services. We conclude that investment incentives are effective in strengthening regional growth and employment in East Germany. Investment-oriented measures should remain a cornerstone of regional policy in the future, with more emphasis given to innovation.

JEL Classification: C23, R11, R58

Keywords: Regional investment incentives, regional growth, panel data

1. Introduction

After reunification, East Germany experienced a short period of high, transfer driven growth that brought its per capita Gross Domestic Product (GDP) from about one-third of the West German level in 1991 to 61 percent in 1997. But with the end of the subsidized boom in construction, convergence came to a standstill for about five years, before progress towards the West German GDP-level resumed at a slow

* Cologne Institute for Economic Research, Konrad-Adenauer-Ufer 21, 50668 Köln, Germany, e-mail: demary@iwkoeln.de.

** *Corresponding author:* Cologne Institute for Economic Research, Capital Office Berlin, Wallstraße 15 / 15a, 10179 Berlin, Germany. E-mail address: roehl@iwkoeln.de.

The authors thank Waltraut Peter, Peggy von Speicher as well as our discussant Klaus-Werner Schatz for their insightful suggestions. Any remaining errors are our own.

pace. Today, 20 years after the fall of the Berlin wall, East Germany has caught up with the west in some aspects while still lagging in most economic indicators.

In 2008, East Germany had less than 16.6 million inhabitants, including 3.4 million residing in Berlin. Focusing on the former German Democratic Republic (GDR) with the eastern part of Berlin, the East German fraction of the total German population has decreased from a fifth in 1990 to less than 18 percent today. And there is no sign that this downward trend is coming to an end. In 2007, the five East German States excluding Berlin had a net loss of 56,100 inhabitants due to migration. An additional contribution to the negative population dynamics are the low birth rates in the eastern states. Its GDP per capita (percent) has only recently surpassed two thirds of the West German level while its unemployment rate is twice the West German rate. But there are favorable signs as well. Among the positive developments are the continuous, substantial growth in the manufacturing sector and the growth of significant industrial clusters in different regions. Overall the structural progress of the East German economy during the past decade is quite remarkable despite its low GDP growth rate. The share of transfer-driven sectors like public and private services is shrinking, while the manufacturing sector is growing strongly. With the continuing convergence of the economic structure, it becomes more and more likely that East Germany will have developed a viable economic structure when the federal "solidarity pact" transfers expire in 2019.

The remainder of this paper is structured as follows. The next section describes the convergence process in East Germany focusing on manufacturing, which has experienced high growth especially in the three southern states. Section three contains an econometric assessment of the effects of regional investment incentives in East Germany. It is shown that financial incentives are an effective policy instrument to stimulate regional growth. Section four concludes, giving some recommendations for the organization of the German regional policy in the future.

2. The Convergence towards West Germany Has Failed So Far – Or Has it Really?

2.1 The State of Convergence

Since 1998, real growth in East Germany has remained below the West German level most of the time. From 1997 to 2001 even per capita growth rates were not higher so that the east-west-relation was stalled at about 60 percent. But since 2002, overall growth reached more or less the western rate in most years and per-capita convergence resumed. In 2008, GDP per capita stood already at 68.5 percent of West Germany's. This convergence of nominal GDP is not only driven by real growth, but also by a process of adjustment of price levels in East and West Germany.[1] In

[1] As regional price levels are not made public by the German statistical office, only nominal values for GDP by region can be compared. Most likely, the East German price level is still

nominal terms, convergence is progressing by about 1 percent of West German GDP per year.

In the nineties, labor cost rose at a high rate in East Germany. As wage increases by far exceeded productivity growth, labor unit cost surpassed West German levels. Companies responded by reducing employment to boost productivity. But since 2000, wages in East Germany have risen only slightly. Because productivity growth was stronger, labor unit cost fell and reached West German levels for the first time in 2007. In manufacturing, they stood at only 87 percent of their West German counterpart (Paque 2008, 5). While investment was a driving force of growth in the nineties, it decreased after 2000 and fell below the West German level in 2005. In 2006, overall investment stood at 77 percent of the West German level with investment in machinery even below this mark. Few investments went into big manufacturing plants in recent years, while a growing share of overall investment has been due to the expansion of small and medium-sized enterprises (SME). Notable exceptions are new plants of the photovoltaic industry, as will be shown in more detail below. While the capital stock per capita and especially research and development (R&D) employment are still far below West German levels, in many other areas like the rate of self-employed people and the formation of new enterprises adjustment has progressed substantially (see table 1). The number of working people remains rather low at 88 percent of the West German level, while labor market participation including unemployed people and commuters to western states is even slightly higher than in the western part of Germany.

In 2008, differences in per-capita GDP between the eastern states were still low, despite their strongly divergent shares of manufacturing and the beginning of the formation of industrial clusters (see below). Two decades after the start of the transformation towards a market economy Saxony's GDP per capita reached the highest level with 22,523 euro[2], while Mecklenburg-Western Pomerania's was the lowest with 21,425 euro. The difference was only 5.1 percent, while the gap between the most affluent and the poorest West German state was 40.2 percent or eight times as high – excluding the city-states. But since 2000, real per-capita growth rates in the eastern states have shown a distinct north-south divide. While Saxony is in the lead with an annualized real growth rate of 2.5 percent, Saxony-Anhalt and Thuringia follow closely with 2.4 percent. The two northern states reached growth rates of between 1 and 2 percent, while Berlin trails behind with a slightly negative growth rate (table 2). The three southern states with manufacturing shares of gross value added (GVA) from 21 to 24 percent have shown higher growth rates than the three northern states recently, but may be affected more strongly by the current crisis. The divergent strength of the manufacturing sector in the East German states and its implications will be discussed in more detail below.

---

lower than the West German level and is rising towards this level and not away from it, implying that east-west-differences since unification were less pronounced than shown statistically.

2 Omitting Berlin, of which only the eastern part belonged to the former GDR.

Table 1

Convergence Indicators

	1991	2000	2008
	West Germany = 100		
Population	25	23	21
GDP[1] per capita	33	60	69[2]
Labor Cost[1]: compensation per dependent employee	49	77	78
Productivity[1]: real GDP per employee	42	69	78
Unit labor costs[1]	119	112	100
Investment per capita	66	110	77[1,2]
Investment in equipment per capita	62	97	62[1,2]
Capital stock per capita	38	64	72[1,3]
Capital stock per employee	40	73	82[1,3]
Export share in manufacturing[1]	52	56	70
R&D employment[1]	49	42	61
Employment share[1]	96	88	88
Share of self emloyed[1]	50	84	100
Unemployment rate	207	239	218[1]
Opening of enterprises	271	87	98[6]
Closure of enterprises	122	92	95[6]

[1] Without Berlin; [2] 2006; [3] 2007; [4] 1999; [5] 2005; [6] Eastern states including Berlin.

Notes: Population is the percentage of East German compared to West German population. The other values give the east-west relation of the indicators, mostly in per capita or per employee terms. Export share is the east-west relation of the respective shares of exports in manufacturing sales. The data are taken from the state level German national accounts, Bundesagentur für Arbeit, Creditreform, Center for Economic Studies (ifo), German statistical office (StBA).

Table 2

Main Economic Indicators of the East German States

	GDP per capita 2008	GDP Growth per capita 2000 to 2008	Manufacturing share in GVA 2008	Unemployment rate 2008	Public debt per capita (as of 2008)
Berlin	25,521	–0.2	12.6	13.9	16,340
Brandenburg	21,649	1.3	15.7	13.0	6,803
Mecklenburg-Western Pomerania	21,425	1.9	13.0	14.1	5,927
Saxony	22,523	2.5	21.0	12.8	2,279
Saxony-Anhalt	22,357	2.4	21.7	14.0	8,259
Thuringia	21,868	2.4	23.7	11.3	6,724
East Germany	22,069	2.2	19.6	13.0	5,490
West Germany	32,205	1.1	24.5	6.4	5,382

Notes: West Germany: without Berlin; Growth per capita is calculated as the real annualized rate from 2000 to 2008. The data are taken from state level German National Accounts, Bundesagentur für Arbeit, Bundesministerium der Finanzen, calculations by authors.

In 2008, Thuringia's rate of unemployment was the lowest of all eastern states at 11.3 percent. In addition to its strong manufacturing sector and high growth rate during the last decade, the state benefited from its geographical location with many employees commuting to Bavaria and Hesse. The highest unemployment rate was measured in Mecklenburg-Western Pomerania with 14.1 percent. Public debt per capita was highest in Saxony-Anhalt, where a stringent fiscal policy after the year 2000 did not suffice to compensate lax policies during the nineties. The higher debt in Berlin cannot be compared, as it comprises communal debt, too. Saxony followed a careful fiscal policy throughout the 18 years since unification and, as a result, its public debt per inhabitant is only a quarter of Saxony-Anhalt's. Relative to the number of inhabitants, all East German states except Saxony already have accumulated higher debts than the West German states on average.

2.2 Adjustment Towards the West German Economic Structure

Though overall convergence is slow, the sectoral structure is adjusting towards the West German structure rather smoothly. The fraction of the construction sector in total gross value added, which was three times as big as that of West Germany in 1995, has now receded to less than 150 percent of the western level. As many East German construction companies are active in the west, an adjustment to 100 percent is unlikely for the near future. The same applies to agriculture, which will remain stronger than in the west because the population density is only 58 percent of West Germany's and agricultural acreage per capita is higher in accordance. Public and private services still account for a higher percentage of gross value added compared to the western states, the east-west relation stands at 130 percent but is receding slowly.

Two important sectors, manufacturing and business-related services, had the lowest percentages in the East German economy as compared to the west throughout the two decades since reunification (see figure 1). But both sectors have been expanding their share since 1992. Business services had a head start in the nineties accounting for two thirds of the West German share in gross value added in 1995 already. Later, its growth rate fell below that of manufacturing. Manufacturing fell to 40 percent of its West German level in GVA in 1992. Due to their low productivity East German manufacturing plants lost their competitiveness and their markets with the introduction of the Deutsche Mark, while new plants and companies had yet to be established. This process took more time than in services. But while the growth of business services petered out after 2000, manufacturing shows a very constant upward trend as a percentage of GVA for the last 15 years. In 2000, it reached 60 percent of the West German share in GVA, and in 2008, already 80 percent. If this rate of structural convergence is maintained, manufacturing will adjust to the West German share in GVA by 2016. In per capita terms, it will of course still be substantially lower as GDP per capita will be, too.

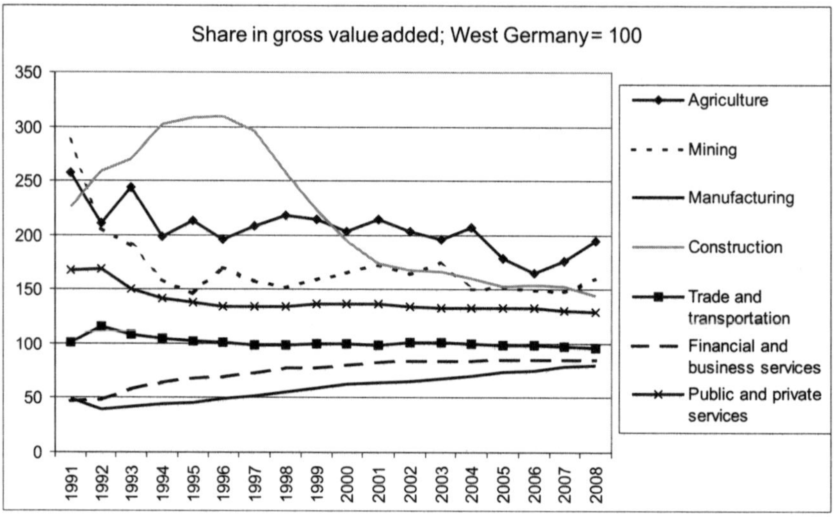

Notes: Excluding Berlin. All data are taken from the state level German national accounts.

Figure 1: Structural Convergence of the East and West German Economies

2.3 Regional Development in Manufacturing

As already shown in the previous section of the paper, in general, the East German states today cannot be characterized as a de-industrialized region like Italy's Mezzogiorno (Sinn 2000). The growth of manufacturing in the last 15 years has driven its share in GVA up to 19.6 percent in 2008, more than in industrialized countries like the United Kingdom (14.4 percent), France (13.2 percent) and the United States (13.2 percent). But the five East German Laender and Berlin show very different levels of industrialization. East Germany's industrial heartlands are located in the southern part with the states Saxony, Thuringia, and the southern region of Saxony-Anhalt. The north with the states of Brandenburg and Mecklenburg-Western Pomerania, the northern part of Saxony-Anhalt and Berlin are much less industrialized by comparison. Figure 2 shows the shares of manufacturing in GVA for the five eastern states, Berlin and West Germany. While Berlin's manufacturing share fell until 2002, in most states it steadily rose from its low point in 1992 until 2008. A marked exception is Mecklenburg-Western Pomerania, where the low mark was reached as late as 1995 and manufacturing growth was lower than in the southern states in most years.

In 1993, the manufacturing shares showed only little divergence ranging from 8.3 percent in Brandenburg to 11.8 percent in Saxony (excluding Berlin). But in 2008, Thuringia led with a share of 23.7 percent, already close to the West German share of 24.5 percent. In Mecklenburg-Western Pomerania, manufacturing had a much lower relevance with only 13 percent of GVA. While Thuringia experienced the fastest growth of the manufacturing sector in the nineties, Saxony-Anhalt has become a kind of an "East German tiger" only after the year 2000. In 2008, its manufacturing share of 21.7 percent even slightly surpassed Saxony's. Saxony-Anhalt's strong manufacturing growth was fuelled by a renaissance of its chemical industry, but also by new plants of photovoltaic panel and wind power plant manufacturers. The formation of two clusters of renewable power industries in the state will be discussed below in more detail.

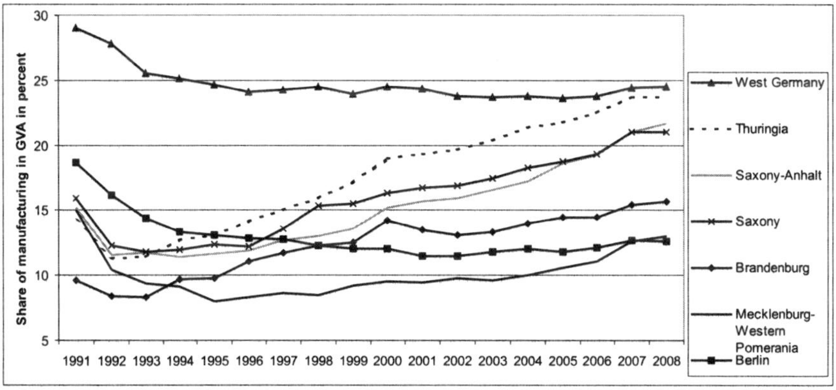

Notes: All data are taken from the state level German national accounts.

Figure 2: Share of Manufacturing in Gross Value Added by State

The strong growth of the manufacturing sector and its share in GVA in the eastern states is not mirrored in a corresponding rise in manufacturing employment. In 1991, the manufacturing employment shares in Saxony and Thuringia were still above 30 percent, which was higher than in West Germany. Labor productivity was below 20 percent of the western level, as many employees were on short time work – sometimes working zero hours. Manufacturing employment did not hit bottom until 1995, when most of the hidden unemployment in manufacturing was converted to open joblessness. Later on, employment rose rather sluggishly in Saxony and Saxony-Anhalt and not at all in Brandenburg and Mecklenburg-Western Pomerania. Only in Thuringia manufacturing employment grew substantially from the late nineties onwards. In 2008, with 20.4 percent of total employment, it even surpassed West Germany's share.

The interaction between the growth of GVA and employment in manufacturing determines the development of labor productivity in the sector. As already mentioned, labor productivity was extremely low after the German unification. With layoffs in the former collective combines and investment in new plants and machinery, productivity started to rise at a fast pace. But substantial labor productivity increases in West German manufacturing in the last two decades have retarded the convergence process. In 2007, only Berlin's small manufacturing sector surpassed

West German productivity levels with 74,944 euro GVA per employee. Saxony-Anhalt was second with 67,380 euros, while Thuringia pays for its strong manufacturing employment in low productivity, trailing the other states. With only 50,529 euro per employee it is still 28 percent below the West German level.

2.4 Shortcomings in High-Tech Industries

Although the structural progress of the East German economy seems quite substantial in comparison to its slow overall growth, there are deficits when it comes to high-tech-industries and important business services. These shortcomings are partly to blame for the lower GDP per capita compared to the west. In West Germany, 2.5 percent of the total workforce is employed in high-tech-industries like electronics and medical technologies, and additionally, 11.2 percent are employed in industries with above-average technological levels like engineering and the chemical, automotive and electrical industries. In East Germany, the numbers are 1.8 percent in high-tech and 5.4 percent in above-average-technology (Titze 2007). In knowledge-intensive services, West Germany leads as well. Especially in financial services, the gap is considerable, with 4.2 percent of total employment compared to only 2 percent in the east. This margin corresponds with the scarcity of head-quarter-functions located in East Germany, as the seats of banks and insurance companies are in West German cities. As these functions contribute to a higher GDP, their absence is detrimental to the convergence process (Blum 2007). The employment share in the R&D sector is marginally higher in the east, with 0.6 percent vs. 0.5 percent in the west. But this only includes employees in separate R&D entities like the limited R&D companies that were formed out of the research laboratories of former collective combines. Most R&D employees are working in manufacturing companies, especially big companies with more than 10,000 employees. In East Germany, there are no companies of this size. Compared to the west, the East German share of R&D employees in the total workforce therefore reaches only 61 percent (table 1).

2.5 The Role of New Industrial Clusters

Despite the aforementioned shortcomings, however, new industries with high growth potential are forming in some East German regions and generate new industrial clusters. The spatial concentration of companies belonging to certain industries connected by supply chains or a common knowledge pool has been thoroughly analyzed in the regional economic literature in the past decade. Braking ground, Porter (1998, 2000) described the main characteristics of industrial clusters. But the term cluster has, nonetheless, remained rather cloudy. In spatial perspective, a cluster can be a city, a region or even a whole country. It can encompass a manufacturing industry or a specific industrial branch or a group of related industries. It can also comprise service industries important to manufacturing (Porter

2000, 254). Despite the uncertainties in the definition given, the concept seems to have merit. Studies of manufacturing industries have shown that companies in cluster regions often grow faster than the industrial average, further strengthening the clusters (Lichtblau et al. 2005).

However, in East Germany industrial clusters are still scarce. Because of the small number of big enterprises the regional "mass" of employment in a specific industry is usually too low to prove empirically the existence of a regional cluster, even if the number of enterprises shows some regional concentration. Using employment data for 2005, Titze (2007, 21) was able to detect only one cluster of a high-tech-industry in an East German region – microelectronics in Dresden. Dresden belonged to Germany's top three regions in this industry's employment, but – excluding Berlin–no other eastern region was able to reach a position among the top seven regions at least. Rosenfeld et al. (2004) show a possibility to adapt the cluster concept to East German reality by looking for enterprise networks etc.

At the start of the clustering process, it is obviously difficult to prove the existence of regional clusters using data only available after a cluster is well established. But there are new clusters forming in industries with very high growth rates, especially the photovoltaic industry. In 2007, this industry employed close to 20,000 people in Germany, 10,000 in the east and a little less in the west (Ruhl and Wackerbauer 2008, 23). In relation to total employment in manufacturing, the East German share of the photovoltaic industry reached 1.2 percent, six times the West German value. While all eastern states boast plants of this highly subsidized new industry, main clusters are located in the Dresden / Freiberg region of Saxony and in Bitterfeld-Wolfen in the south of Saxony-Anhalt. In 2008, photovoltaic employment in East Germany had already risen to 14,000, according to the IWH enterprise panel (Brachert and Hornych 2009, 89). The Dresden-Freiberg cluster has a share of about 30 percent of these, while the Bitterfeld-Wolfen cluster has a share of 25 percent and a smaller cluster located in Thuringia's Erfurt region 14 percent. But the future development of this industry is highly dependent on the conditions of German and international subsidies to promote renewable energies. Closer to delivering energy at market prices are wind power plants. In this industry, there are two potential clusters in East Germany based on plants of big West German enterprises. The regions chosen for the establishment of these plants – Magdeburg and Rostock – are not located in southern East Germany. But these investments are much more like satellites of their West German parent companies than the photovoltaic enterprises, with limited potential for rapid cluster growth.

While industrial clusters seem to stimulate the growth of enterprises through urbanization, localization and network economies, their value as a goal of regional policy measures is dubious. Successful clusters have to be big – but political decision makers in state capitals have to weigh the interests of all regions within their states to win elections. In Brandenburg, the state government defined 65 potential industrial clusters, where investments in certain industries are to be favored by special conditions, including the joint task federal-state incentives to strengthen the regional economic structure (Titze 2007, 31). This policy of differentiated industry-specific incentives goes far beyond the scope of the cluster concept. Alecke and Untiedt (2007) criticize the overambitious goals of a regional policy which tries to control private investment decisions by public planners, stressing the informational deficits of the planning authorities. Demands for the concentration of investment incentives on industrial clusters (e.g. Dohnanyi and Most 2004) seem to be done in ignorance of the fact that the support through the joint task is already highly concentrated, with a few – and not the poorest – regions in East Germany receiving the bulk of the funds (Röhl 2005).

More promising for the generation of innovative clusters are indirect measures like bolstering universities and colleges, subsidies for R&D and network building between enterprises, educational institutions, and public actors like regional authorities. But not all relevant industries are high-tech. In poor regions with high unemployment, local industries are predominantly low or middle tech. These enterprises and industries cannot be ignored, if the regions' economies are to become more successful. The joint task supports investments of manufacturing enterprises in the East German states not only in high tech industries, although they are more likely to receive substantial funds. But generally, a differentiation is intended along the lines of enterprise size and regional prosperity. These privileges in regard to the amount of investment subsidies do not favor more affluent cluster regions in East Germany (with bigger, more technology-oriented companies), but their effect seems to be marginal in relation to the concentration of overall subsidies through the regional pattern of enterprise investment decisions (Röhl 2005). In general, enterprises can find an optimal location for their investment decisions without guidance by public planners, recognizing the advantages of clusters.

3. Regional Investment Incentives in East Germany – Does the Joint Task Work?

Regional policy in Germany intends to reduce regional inequality through measures to raise the income levels in poor regions. 40 years ago, the system of the joint task to strengthen the economic structure in poor regions by means of investment incentives was started in West Germany. Although its success in supporting poor regions was discussed controversially, the joint task was transferred to East Germany after unification. Investment incentives seemed to be the best way to quickly bring the low East German per capita capital stock up to the West German level. Reduced cost for capital were supposed to stimulate investors to shift production into East German regions (Alecke and Untiedt 2000, 174, Eckey and Kosfeld 2004), thus creating additional employment opportunities. But at the same time, the production factor capital becomes less expensive in relation to the factor labor (Sinn 2000). Because of this, regional income might rise, while employment growth lags behind.

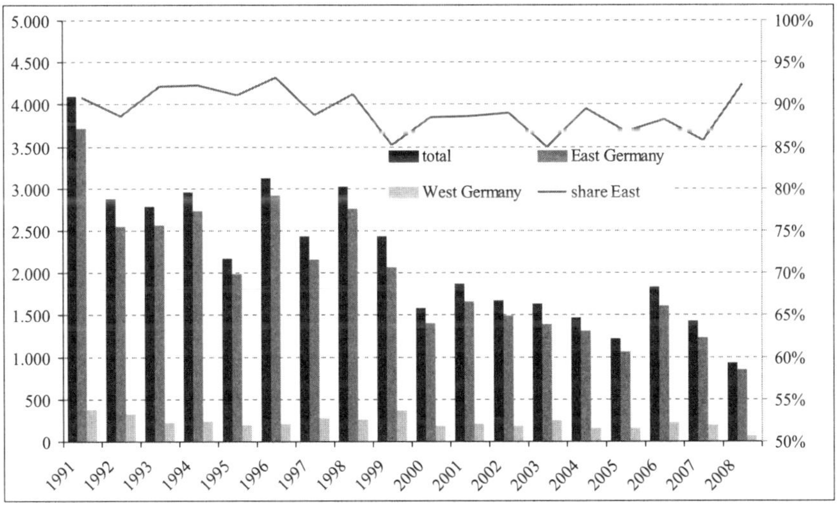

Notes: The plotted data are based on the dataset on joint task investment incentives provided by the Bundesamt für Wirtschaft und Ausfuhrkontrolle (BAFA).

Figure 3: The Distribution of Joint Task Investment Incentives on East and West Germany – in Billion Euros, 1991 to 2008

The amount of investment subsidies given to investors in East Germany since unification is quite large. From 1991 to 2008, almost 36 billion euros were handed out in the joint task alone, co-financing investments of 173 billion euro in manufacturing (and a few related services).[3] The program frame of the joint task now in force is valid until 2013. At that time it has to be evaluated and adjusted again.

3.1 A Panel Data Regression Model for East German Regions

As already shown, manufacturing growth can be counted as a success story in the rather cumbersome convergence process of the East German economy. But to what extent are the investment incentives of the joint task driving this positive development? To give an answer to this question, we will present results of a panel regression for the East German regions, represented by 113 districts (Kreise). Data on GVA in manufacturing is taken from the German national accounts (Volkswirtschaftliche Gesamtrechnung) on district level, while data on investment incentives is available on the firm level. This data set consisting of firm level financial incentives is not released to the public but was provided to us by the Bundesamt für Wirtschaft und Ausfuhrkontrolle, a German federal agency which collects and administers this

3 In addition to this, the federal government gives a guaranteed investment allowance of 12.5 to 25 percent (depending on enterprise size).

data. From these firm level data we aggregated the volume of the incentives for each of the 113 districts by year.[4] We are using an up-to-date data set for our empirical assessment of the performance of regional financial incentives in Eastern Germany. This contrasts to earlier evaluations of regional policy measures in Eastern Germany, where only data for short periods since unification were available. To account for the strong differences in economic structure occurring between cities, agglomerated regions and the periphery, we defined four different types of regions. Theses types, (primary) cities, conurbations around the most important cities, secondary cities and peripheral regions, are distributed as shown in Figure 4.

Our regression model decomposes the logarithmic regional gross value added in manufacturing y into an autonomous trend component t related to factors different from subsidization and common to all regions and a region-specific component which is related to the logarithmic regional volume of incentives s. In line with the current literature (see, e.g., Schalk and Untied 2000) on the performance of regional policy measures we assume a lag of three years for investment incentives to have an effect on gross value added. A sensitivity analysis showed that this assumption seems to be realistic in terms of significance of the estimated coefficient. In formal terms, the model looks as follows

$$y_{it} = d_1\alpha_1 + d_2\alpha_2 + d_3\alpha_3 + d_4\alpha_4 + \beta_1 t + \beta_2 s_{i,t-3} + \varepsilon_{it} ,$$

where the time trend t represents the autonomous growth component, while s is the growth component of region i at time t which is related to subsidization. This decomposition is based on the fact that it is the easiest way of decomposing the effects of subsidization from other growth components of gross value added under the restriction that other growth components were not available as data sets on the regional level. A shortcoming of this method is that we might overestimate the size of the trend growth and the effect of investment incentives to economic growth, but in our view it is the best compromise between having a rich disaggregated dataset and having lots of explanatory factors. The decomposition of gross value added into an autonomous growth component and a component related to subsidization can also be justified by econometric reasons, because it controls for unit roots in the data generating process. Conventional panel unit-root tests indicate mixed results on the stationarity or non-stationarity properties of gross-value added. The finding of the rejection of a unit-root in gross value added can be due to the short time horizon of the sample. Because gross value added time series normally follow unit root processes the introduction of a time trend might control for possible non-stationarities in the data.

---

4 Aggregation was necessary because financial aids are not reported on district level, while gross value added is not reported on the firm level.

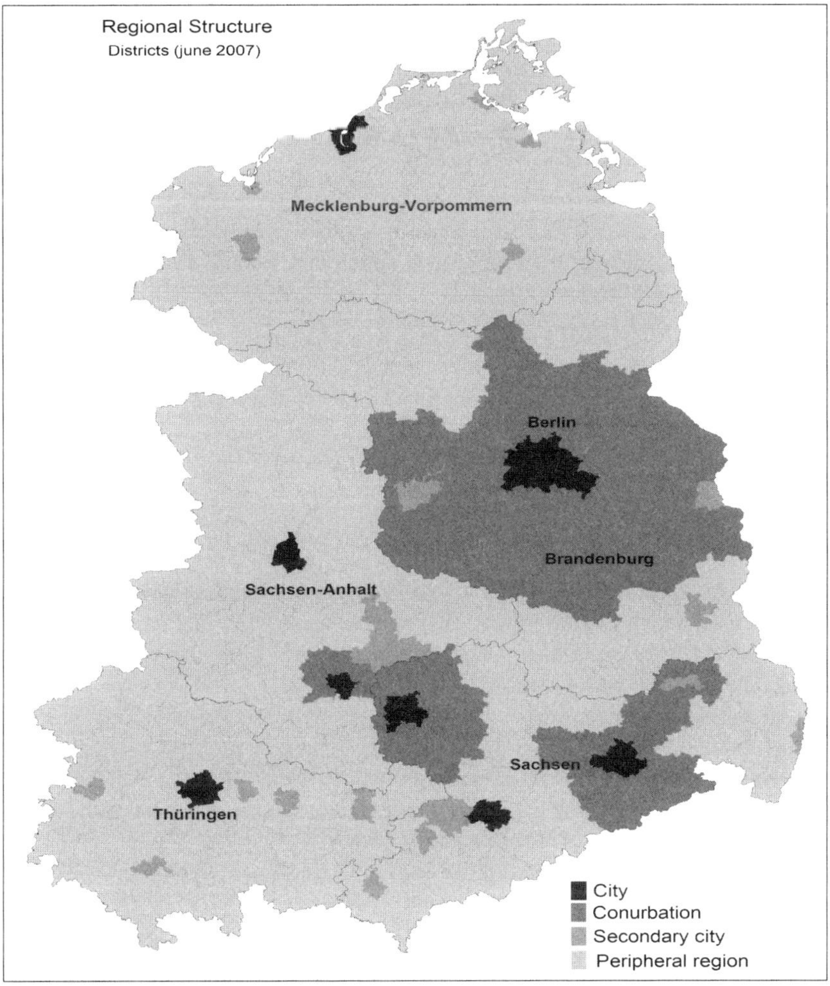

Note: Regions (district level) classified by authors.

Figure 4: The Spatial Structure of East German Regions

We transformed the data to logarithms before estimating the model. Thus, the coefficient before the time trend t can be interpreted as the long-run average percentage growth rate over all regions, while the coefficient before the subsidies can be interpreted as an elasticity. Thus, this elasticity measures the *ceteris paribus* percentage growth in GVA due to a one percentage growth in subsidies. To account for the heterogeneity in the four regional types which differ in average gross value added size we introduce region-type-specific fixed effects which we model by a particular dummy variable d for each regional type. Thus, we use a special form of a least squares dummy variable model. With this approach we pool regions in each region type which is from a modeling perspective not problematic because regions of each type are more or less similar in economic structure and size. Moreover, we want to concentrate on region-group specific effects and not on regional effects. Note that we assume the same autonomous growth in gross value added for all regions. Although this might seem to be restrictive, it is a sensible assumption because there might be growth factors which are common to all regions which are summarized in this term while we assume that regional investment incentives are the region-specific growth components. Moreover, model variations that assume different growth paths for all regions were not found to be statistically significant.

In an alternative model formulation we try to account for individual heterogeneity by assuming that each region type responds differently to an increase in subsidies. In econometric terms this heterogeneity can be introduced by the following model variation

$$\begin{aligned} y_{it} &= d_1\alpha_1 + d_2\alpha_2 + d_3\alpha_3 + d_4\alpha_4 + \beta_1 t \\ &\quad + d_1\beta_2 s_{i,t-3} + d_2\beta_3 s_{i,t-3} + d_3\beta_4 s_{i,t-3} + d_4\beta_5 s_{i,t-3} + \varepsilon_{it} \, . \end{aligned}$$

Within this specification we allow for an additional size effect in the gross value added response to a higher volume of investment incentives as measured by the different elasticities. Note, that this model specification nests the former model as a special case if we assume all elasticities to be equal. In other words we assume that the regional incentives have different impacts in different regional types. Thus, within this more general model framework we are able to perform a statistical test for testing the hypothesis that subsidization has different effects in different regional types. This can be done by comparing the general model 2 with its restricted version which is model 1. Under the null hypothesis

$$H_0 : \beta_2 = \beta_3 = \beta_4 = \beta_5$$

subsidies have the same contribution to manufacturing growth in all region types, while rejection of this null hypothesis indicates that the effects of subsidies to growth is region-type-specific in East-Germany. This test can easily be performed as an F-test, which is in our case $F(3,1231)$-distributed.

3.2 Empirical Results for Regions

In this part of the paper we present the empirical results on the effects of regional investment incentives in Eastern Germany based on the models presented before.

Table 3

Regression Results for Manufacturing Gross Value Added: Model 1

	Estimated coefficient
City	1.432** (4.637)
Conurbation	0.564 (1.742)
Secondary city	0.350 (1.150)
Peripheral region	0.243 (0.760)
Investment incentive	0.288** (15.454)
Time trend	0.064** (12.644)
Goodness of fit	0.428

Notes: The region types city, conurbation, secondary city and peripheral region are modeled by dummy variables. Because the data is transformed to logarithms the coefficient for investment incentive volume can be interpreted as an elasticity, while the time trend can be interpreted as a balanced growth rate. Values of the t – statistic corresponding to the null hypothesis that the coefficient is zero are reported in parenthesis. The asterisks * and ** indicate significance of a level of 5 and 1 percent. The panel consists of 113 regional observations spanning the time from 1996 to 2006.

Table 3 contains the regression results for model one, for which we assume that the effects of regional investment subsidies are common to all regions and that there is an autonomous growth factor common to all regions. The results indicate a long-run growth path of 6 percent per year for the autonomous growth component, which is statistically significant. This is the average growth of every region not related to subsidization. The reason that this growth rate seems to be very high – higher than actual average manufacturing growth – can be due to missing additional explanatory variables. The elasticity of regional financial support on gross value added is 0.288, indicating that an increase in investment incentive volume of one percent leads to a growth in manufacturing GVA of 0.288 percent. If we reformulate the model and allow individual fixed effects, this coefficient decreases in size. However, it remains positive and significant. The fact that this coefficient is positive and significantly different from zero is an indication that regional investment incentives have effects in stimulating regional growth. However, this finding is just evidence for the effectiveness of this policy instrument. In order to analyze its efficiency one has to perform a cost-benefit analysis. In a model variation with individual fixed effects the estimated elasticities were lower, but remained positive and highly significant. One shortcoming of this model is that the effects of regional incentives are assumed to be equal across the four regional types. Therefore, we decompose this elasticity into four region-specific elasticities as described before in the general regression model (table 4).

Table 4

Regression Results for Gross Value Added in Manufacturing: Model 2

	Estimated Coefficient	
City	–0.680	(–0.437)
Conurbation	2.841**	(5.143)
Secondary city	0.855	(1.834)
Peripheral region	–0.141	(–0.320)
Elasticities of investment incentive in:		
City	0.415**	(4.387)
Conurbation	0.151**	(4.646)
Secondary city	0.257**	(8.588)
Peripheral region	0.313**	(11.830)
Time trend	0.061**	(12.200)
Goodness of fit	0.435	
F-Test on equal elasticities	6.153	(0.000)

Notes: The region-types city, conurbation, secondary city and peripheral regions are modeled by dummy-variables. Because the data is transformed to logarithms the coefficient for regional incentives can be interpreted as an elasticity, while the time trend can be interpreted as a balanced growth rate. Values of the *t*-statistic corresponding to the null hypothesis that the coefficient is zero are reported in parenthesis. The asterisks * and ** indicate significance of a level of 5 and 1 percent. The panel consists of 113 regional observations spanning the time from 1996 to 2006.

Table 4 contains regression results for the more general model in which we allow the investment incentive elasticities to be region-type-specific. What can be seen is that this assumption does not change the main model predictions. The time trend remains significant indicating an autonomous common balanced growth of six percent per year for the manufacturing sector, which is statistically significant. The elasticities change from 0.288, which we estimated for model specification 1, to 0.415 for (primary) cities, to 0.151 for conurbations adjoining the big cities, to 0.257 for secondary cities and 0.313 for peripheral regions. All four estimates are significantly different from zero. Moreover, the *F*-test indicates that the four elasticities are significantly different from each other. From these results we can conclude that investment incentives have different effects in the four region types. The results show that the largest effects of investment incentives on gross value added in manufacturing is achieved in the important cities and in peripheral regions, while we measure the lowest effects in conurbations. A possible reason for this result is the proximity of the conurbated regions to big cities, where most of the secondary effects of the investments realized in the conurbations might occur. Note that we already controlled for region-type-specific effects by the four dummy variables for the constant thus indicating that there are genuine region type specific effects of the investment incentives. All in all, the empirical results indicate that there are significant positive effects of regional policy measures on sectoral GVA in East Germany.

3.3 Industry-Specific Empirical Results

In this subsection we employ the same methodology as in the subsection before in order to explain employment effects of region-specific investment incentives in East Germany. Employment data are available for manufacturing industries on the district level. We enlarge our empirical investigation by running the regressions explained in the former sections by using industry specific employment instead of gross values added as the variable to be explained by the model. Thus, we are able to generate datasets for 113 regions spanning the years from 1998 to 2007 for 17 industries in manufacturing and business services supported by the joint task. In order to shorten the table we only report the estimated elasticities and skip the fixed effects and the trend growth component in employment. This information can be provided by the authors on request.

Table 5

Employment Effects of Regional Investment Incentives

	Estimated Coefficient	Goodness of fit (R^2)
Food products, tobacco (WZ-no. 15 – 16)	0.086** (6.596)	0.339
Textiles and leather products (WZ-no. 17 – 19)	0.389** (10.118)	0.258
Wood, Paper and products thereof (WZ-no. 20 – 22)	0.164** (10.572)	0.368
Chemicals and chemical products (WZ-no. 23 – 25)	0.239** (11.826)	0.194
Non-metallic mineral products (WZ-no. 26)	0.147** (6.658)	0.132
Metals and metal products (WZ-no. 27 – 28)	0.227** (19.104)	0.395
Machinery (WZ-no. 29)	0.140** (8.631)	0.296
Office machinery, radio and communication equipment (WZ-no. 30,32)	0.226** (5.420)	0.306
Electrical machinery (WZ-no. 31)	0.207** (5.904)	0.249
Medical, precision and optical instruments (WZ-no. 33)	0.204** (9.105)	0.423
Motor vehicles (WZ-no. 34)	0.162** (3.819)	0.131
Other transport equipment (WZ-no. 35)	0.134** (1.881)	0.207
Furniture (WZ-no. 36)	0.185** (7.715)	0.262
Recycling (WZ-no. 37)	0.053** (1.198)	0.254
Computer services (WZ-no. 72)	0.119** (3.870)	0.623
Research and development (WZ-no. 73)	0.284** (4.016)	0.465
Other business services (WZ-no. 74)	0.037** (3.088)	0.717

Notes: The region-types city, conurbation, secondary city and peripheral regions are modeled by dummy-variables (not reported). Because the data is transformed to logarithms the coefficient for investment incentives can be interpreted as an elasticity, while the time trend can be interpreted as a balanced growth rate (not reported). Values of the *t*-statistic corresponding to the null hypothesis that the coefficient is zero are reported in parenthesis. The asterisks * and ** indicate significance of a level of 5 and 1 percent. The panel consists of 113 regional observations spanning the time from 1998 to 2007.

From this table can be inferred that the largest impact of regional investment incentives on employment can be found in the industries textiles, metals, office machinery and communication equipment, electrical machinery, medical and precision instruments and R&D. The results indicate, with some exceptions, that financial support has the strongest effects on employment in labor and human-capital-intensive industries.[5] But all estimated coefficients are significantly different from zero and positive. Thus, regional investment incentives have significant employment effects in East Germany for all industries under consideration.

4. Conclusions

Prima facie, the convergence of the East German economy towards the West German level of prosperity seems to be stalled. Real growth in the east did not surpass the western growth rate substantially for about a decade. But in spite of this, nominal GDP per capita is still converging, standing now at 69 percent of the West German level after only 60 percent in 2000.

After fears in the nineties that East Germany would become a de-industrialized region, like the Italian Mezzogiorno, manufacturing has had a strong comeback with healthy growth rates that brought its share in gross value added up from below 11 percent in 1993 to 19.6 percent in 2008. But there is a distinctive north-south-divide with the manufacturing share in the southern states almost reaching the West German average while lagging behind substantially in the northern states. This development mirrors the spatial structure observed before World War II.

In the second part of this paper, the contribution of investment incentives of the joint regional policy task to manufacturing growth was evaluated using three versions of a panel regression model. It was shown that the investment incentives had a significant effect on manufacturing value added and employment on a regional level, playing an important role in the renaissance of East German manufacturing.

But despite the encouraging growth of the manufacturing sector, deficits concerning the share of high-tech-industries, big enterprises, headquarter functions and industrial clusters remain. Headquarter functions and financial services are clustered in big agglomerations, of which East Germany has only one, the capital Berlin. But a tendency to move high-value functions to Berlin (or smaller East German cities) has not been observed since unification, implying that East Germany will remain devoid of them for time to come. Because of this, a prosperity level like that measured in the poorer West German states like Schleswig-Holstein and Lower Saxony[6] is a more realistic goal than the West German average. Even this goal demands

---

[5] Note however, that spillover effects in other industries and regions, which are likely to be higher in capital-intensive industries, are not included in this model.

[6] In 2008, the GDP per capita of the poorest West German states amounted to 82 to 83 percent of the West German average.

considerable progress in productivity that is usually observed in bigger production units. With ongoing growth in manufacturing, East German SME could be able to grow into higher size classes, filling the gap in the long run. As investment incentives were shown to be an effective instrument to foster manufacturing growth in East Germany, the incentives granted under the joint task regional policy scheme should be continued after the current program frame ends in 2013. At that time, also the guaranteed investment allowance ("Investitionszulage") given in addition to the joint federal-state incentives is phased out. This can be seen as an opportunity to concentrate regional incentives in the joint task program, which should be

- adequately funded. With the end of the additional investment allowance, regional policy would be in danger of becoming marginalized without funding on at least the current scale
- not over-selective. A concentration on a few industries and clusters is encouraged by some authors, but this would strain the capabilities of public planners and diminish the abilities of enterprise leaders to find an adequate location for their investments (inside the bigger region which is supported) without public intervention[7]
- more innovation-oriented. Investments in R&D instead of equipment should be supported more strongly. This holds at least as long as there is no general R&D-related incentive like a tax allowance. Instruments like Pro Inno and its successor do not have a broad scope. Only a small fraction of all companies is supported by current programs supporting innovation.

Most incentives for investment and R&D activity are restricted to SME with less than 250 employees, according to European Union directives. But manufacturing enterprises of between 250 and 1.000 employees are often too small to compete against bigger companies in international markets. Because of this, measures in support of R&D and innovations in general should not be constrained to small enterprises with less than 250 employees, but comprise also medium enterprises bigger than that (IW Consult 2006). Otherwise, there might be a barrier to further enterprise growth above the narrow EU definition of SME, which would be problematic for East Germany because of the scarcity of big enterprises.

References

Alecke, B. / *Untiedt,* G. (2007): "Clusterförderung und Wirtschaftspolitik – 'Heilsbringer' oder 'Wolf im Schafspelz'?" List Forum für Wirtschafts- und Finanzpolitik 33 (2), 89 – 105.

Blum, U. (2007): "Der Einfluss von Führungsfunktionen auf das Regionaleinkommen: eine ökonometrische Analyse deutscher Regionen," IWH Wirtschaft im Wandel 6 / 2007, 187 – 194.

---

7 As was shown in Röhl (2005), the regional distribution of the joint task incentives is highly concentrated even without an explicit decision to support clusters.

Brachert, M. / *Hornych,* C. (2009): "Die Formierung von Photovoltaik-Clustern in Ostdeutschland," IWH Wirtschaft im Wandel 2 / 2009, 81 – 90.

Dohnanyi, K. v. / *Most,* E. (2004): "Kurskorrektur des Aufbau Ost," Berlin, Report for "Gesprächskreis Ost" of the German Federal Government.

Eckey, H.-F. / *Kosfeld,* R. (2004): "Regionaler Wirkungsgrad und räumliche Ausstrahlungseffekte der Investitionsförderung," Volkswirtschaftliche Diskussionsbeiträge der Universität Kassel 55 / 04.

IW Consult (2006): "Forschungsförderung in Deutschland: Stimmen Angebots- und Nachfragebedingungen für den Mittelstand?," Study for Stiftung Industrieforschung, Authors: Elsenbast, W., K. Lichtblau and K.-H. Röhl, Köln.

Lichtblau, K. / *Neligan,* A / *Richter,* I. (2005): "Erfolgsfaktoren von M+E-Clustern in Deutschland," IW-Trends 32 (2), 31 – 44.

Paqué, K.-H. (2008): "Transformationspolitik in den neuen Ländern: Eine industrielle Erfolgsgeschichte?," Presentation at the Annual Meeting of the Institut der deutschen Wirtschaft Köln, October, 22, 2008, Königswinter.

Porter, M. E. (1998), "Location, Clusters, and the 'New' Microeconomics of Competition," Business Economics, January, 7 – 13.

– (2000): "Locations, Clusters, and Company Strategy," in The Oxford Handbook of Economic Geography, edited by G. L. Clark, M. P. Feldman, and M. S. Gertler, Oxford, 253 – 274.

Röhl, K.-H. (2005): "Entwicklung und Schwerpunkte der Regionalförderung in Deutschland," IW-Trends 32 (1), 17 – 32.

– (2008): "Sind Strukturhilfen sinnvoll?," WISU 3 / 08, 269 – 270.

– (2009): "Strukturelle Konvergenz der ostdeutschen Wirtschaft," IW-Trends 36 (1), 67 – 81.

Rosenfeld, M. T. / *Franz,* P. / *Günther,* J., et al. (2004): "Innovative Kompetenzfelder, Produktionsnetzwerke und Branchenschwerpunkte der ostdeutschen Wirtschaft," Research Project for Bundesamt für Bauwesen und Raumordnung, Final Report, Halle / Saale.

Ruhl, V. / *Wackerbauer,* J. (2008): "Struktur und Entwicklungspotential der Photovoltaikindustrie in Deutschland," ifo Schnelldienst 14 / 2008, 14 – 28.

Schalk, H. J. / *Untiedt,* G. (2000): "Regional investment incentives in Germany: Impact on factor demand and growth," The Annals of Regional Science 34, 173 – 195.

Sinn, H.-W. (2000): "Germany's Economic Unification, An Assessment after Ten Years," CESifo Working Paper 247.

Titze, M. (2007): "Strategien der neuen Bundesländer im Rahmen der Gemeinschaftsaufgabe, 'Verbesserung der regionalen Wirtschaftsstruktur' – Ein Vergleich," IWH-Diskussionspapiere 14.

Twenty Years after the Fall of the Berlin Wall: Structural Convergence in a Slow-Growth Environment

Comment

By Klaus-Werner Schatz*

Has German unification become an economic success or was it a failure? This is the question with which the authors deal in their paper, above all in the first part, on which I shall focus here, concentrating on the developments since the end of the 1990s, as they seem to give reason for concern.

1. Macroeconomic East-West Convergence

The east-west convergence was without any doubt more rapid in the 1990s than in the following years, no matter which indicator is taken into consideration. The conclusion is often that the initially strong impulse for the East to catch up with the West is now fading, and that development in the East is hovering. As I see it, the authors do not openly share this argument. Yet, they say that the convergence of the East German welfare level to West German levels seems to be stalled. They argue that real economic growth of the East German economy has not surpassed the western growth rate for about a decade now. I should like to draw the attention to the fact that at the same time, real gross domestic product (GDP) per inhabitant (per capita) has increased by one-fifth in the East and by just one-tenth in the West. Thereby, nominal East German GDP per capita has risen from 60 percent of the West German level in the year 2000 to 69 percent at present, as the authors themselves mention. Hence, in the East both the absolute and the relative welfare level continued to increase substantially in recent years, and I cannot see stagnation.

2. East Germany: Catching up by the Migration of its Population?

It is often objected that the rise of per-capita GDP in the new federal states is a result of their population decline caused by the migration of elderly people beyond working age, of employed persons with a low productivity and income, and of the

* Honorary Professor, University of Kiel. Mailing address: Klaus Werner Schatz, Vordere Wurth 6, 24161 Altenholz. E-mail: Klaus-Werner.Schatz@gmx.de.

unemployed. Also, low birth rates have contributed to the population decrease. Hence, welfare gains are said not to stem from active policy measures pushing regional growth ahead, but from passive policy resulting in a higher average productivity among the remaining work force and in increased per capita GDP.[1] Röhl and Demary apparently consider the decrease of the population a negative trend.

In the new federal states, GDP per capita made up for 69 percent of the level in the old states last year. From the year 2000 to 2008 the number of inhabitants has decreased by 800 million persons (or 5.8 percent) in the East. If the population size had been the same last year as in 2000 with the GDP of 2008, per capita income would have been 6 percent lower in East Germany and would have made up only 65 percent of the level in West Germany. This is a noticeable difference, and thus claims of catching up through migration seem to be justified at least partly. In contrast, the size and the importance of the (net-)migration of labor force participants (0.120 million persons) are often far overestimated. If this migration had not occurred, relative GDP per capita would have been only one percentage point higher in 2008, making up 70 percent instead of 69 percent of the West German level.

Instead, the increase in labor productivity was decisive for the rise of GDP per capita. If the GDP per employed person had remained on the level attained in the year 2000, per capita income would have accounted for only 61 percent of the western level in 2008 instead of 69 percent.

3. Structural Convergence

The authors deal in detail with structural convergence, here in particular with the manufacturing sector.[2] Yet, what does structural convergence stand for? Is it an

1 In the sense discussed here, passive policy should not be rejected per se, neither from a regional nor from an overall economic point of view. It may well be that meaningful opportunities for active policy do not exist and that any investment should be undertaken instead in other parts of the country offering jobs with higher productivity for persons who migrate. However, it is also argued that GDP growth has been dampened by migration as many highly qualified persons left the East and went to the West. The component analysis undertaken here does not allow us to deal with such details. It enables us to analyze only whether migration has contributed to per capita GDP increases or to decreases.

2 In contrast to what may be expected (net-)migration was not more significant in the new member states with a smaller manufacturing sector. In Brandenburg manufacturing contributes substantially less (16 percent) to Gross Value Added (GVA) than in the average of the eastern states (20 percent). But its population remained practically constant between 1991 and 2008. Mecklenburg-Western Pomerania has the smallest manufacturing industry accounting for a GVA share of only 13 percent, and it has lost 12 percent of its inhabitants since 1991. Yet, in Saxony with a manufacturing share of 21 percent the losses have been of a similar size (11 percent). In Thuringia, where manufacturing ranks at the top (24 percent) among the new member states, population losses have been as significant as in Mecklenburg-Western Pomerania. Saxony-Anhalt, which keeps the second place with regard to the importance of manufacturing (22 percent), ranks at the first place with regard to population losses (16 percent).

analytical concept or is it utilized in a normative sense? What does it mean if the structure of the East German economy fails to adjust to that in West Germany? Does the quality of an economic policy depend on its ability to achieve the adjustment of economic structures?

Obviously, the authors attribute high importance to adjustment of the weight of the manufacturing sector–its contribution to overall economic value added – to the West German level for achieving the convergence of per capita incomes. Apparently it is assumed that with a fast-growing manufacturing sector, the growth rate of GDP will be high, that with a bigger weight of the manufacturing sector the GDP per inhabitant will be higher, and that only with the same contribution of the manufacturing sector to value added as in the West will it be possible for the East to achieve the western welfare level. Here, Röhl and Demary obviously share the view that remaining differences in income are due above all to the insufficient adjustment of economic structures in East Germany to structures in West Germany. Possibly, it is the permanent reference to West Germany which leads to the belief that the same weight of the manufacturing sector as in the old federal states must be aimed at allowing for the same welfare level in the new federal states.

Empirical evidence does not at all support the notion that with a bigger contribution of manufacturing to value added incomes per capita will be higher. In many countries, the contribution of manufacturing is significantly lower than in the old federal states or in the new ones, either. In these countries, the income level is not necessarily lower and in many cases is even substantially higher. Röhl and Demary do not neglect to mention these international observations. But, to me it seems that they do not draw adequate conclusions. In addition, the contribution of manufacturing to value added differs among the old German federal states (excluding the city states Berlin, Bremen, and Hamburg) significantly as well. These differences do not correspond with differences in income levels (all figures for 2008). The contribution is the lowest (at 19 percent) in Hesse, where GDP per capita is the highest (at € 36,400) among the states. Rhineland-Palatinate ranks in third place with regard to the contribution to value added (at 26 percent), but only in seventh place (at € 26,600) in the income hierarchy. It is obvious, too, that the authors have some difficulties dealing with the observation that in East Germany the differences in GDP per capita still are substantially smaller than the differences in the contribution of manufacturing to value added.

In 2008, the share of manufacturing in domestic gross value added accounted for 19.6 percent in the new federal states, making up 80 percent of the level in the old federal states. If, in the new federal states, the share had been 24.5 percent and therefore as high as in the old states at present, the income level of East Germany would have been just 1 percent higher than it actually is. The relative East German income level in comparison to the West would increase on a similar order. Taken together, this means that pursuing the adjustment of structures is not very meaningful.

4. Implications

Röhl and Demary write that deficits in high-tech industries and in business services can partly help to explain the continuing income differences between East and West Germany. I agree, but this is, as they say, just part of the explanation. While Saxony's income level ranks at the top of the new federal states, it makes up for only 87 percent of the level in Schleswig-Holstein, which is the lowest among the old federal states. In Saxony, the share of manufacturing in gross value added is significantly higher than in Schleswig-Holstein; the value added per person employed, however, is substantially lower. These observations can be summarized by concluding that labor productivity is higher in Schleswig-Holstein than in Saxony. But that explains little.

Röhl and Demary write that "due to their low productivity East German manufacturing plants lost their competitiveness and their markets with the introduction of the Deutsche Mark." Gerhard Schürer, then Head of the State Central Planning Commission of the German Democratic Republic (GDR), has provided a case illustrating the core of the problem and what really mattered (Schürer 1989). Within the previous Council for Mutual Economic Assistance (COMECON), the GDR was in charge of the production of certain types of microelectronic components. The production of one 256 kilobyte memory chip entailed costs of 536 East German marks. Such chips could have been acquired at a fraction of these costs from the world market, namely at a price of 6 marks. This can, of course, be translated into low productivity in the production of chips in the GDR. However, measures aiming to increase productivity would have been useless. After the breakdown of the GDR, the challenge was not to gradually increase productivity in the existing production plants; rather, the whole economy had to be converted and integrated into the global economy, with new products overnight.

The privatization of the previous state-owned companies, the investments that accompanied privatization, and other investments have pushed the process ahead. Yet, too few industrial clusters exist. Clusters are important as they promise repeated generation of new products, allowing the income level to increase. The authors report that the continued existence of clusters in a number of cases even depends on permanent subsidization.

The West German economy is deeply and broadly marked by globalization and by experiences of globalization. The many small and medium-sized companies in manufacturing and in downstream and upstream industrial sectors have acquired knowledge, which cannot be available to the same extent in East Germany. In the old federal states, companies have been in business much longer, and in addition they cover a much broader spectrum of the economy and are more deeply involved with other businesses. The disadvantaged position of the new federal states will gradually fade away, as over time, experience will be gained, the number of small and medium sized companies will increase, and the field in which they are active will become broader.

References

Schürer, G. (1989): "Überlegungen zur weiteren Arbeit am Volkswirtschaftsplan 1989 und darüber hinaus," in Vor dem Bankrott der DDR. Dokumente des Politbüros des ZK der SED aus dem Jahre 1988 zum Scheitern der Einheit von Wirtschafts- und Sozialpolitik (Die Schürer / Mittag-Kontroverse) Mit einem Gespräch mit Gerhard Schürer, ehem. Mitglied des Politbüros und Vorsitzender der Staatlichen Plankommission der DDR," Hans-Hermann Hertle. Berliner Arbeitshefte zur sozialwissenschaftlichen Forschung 63, Berlin, August 1991, Dokumentation XXIV.

Is There a Growing Risk of Old-Age Poverty in East Germany?

By Stefan Krenz*, Wolfgang Nagl**, and Joachim Ragnitz***

Abstract

Is old-age poverty becoming a serious problem in Germany? Long-term unemployment and increasing disruptions in employment biographies induce shrinking retirement arrangements. We analyze the income security through the statutory pension scheme, which is still the most important income source for pensioners. Therefore we develop a micro-simulation-model to compare the situation of new retirees in 2020 – 2022 to those in 2004 – 2006. We do this for the most common household-types in East and West Germany in respect to gender and education in order to find specific differences. For both parts of Germany education is the key to a sufficient statutory pension. The currently higher average pensions in East Germany will decrease over time. In general, the probability of old-age poverty increases. Our findings help to clarify the risk of post-retirement poverty for specific household constellations.

JEL Classification: I32, J 11, J14

Keywords: statutory pension system, old-age poverty risk, pension distribution, micro-simulation model

1. Introduction

Every now and then there is a public and political debate about a growing old-age poverty risk in East Germany. Besides other arguments, there are two points one has to consider seriously: demographic change and the difficult labor market situation in East Germany after reunification. Talking about demographic change, the main point is the increasing proportion of retired people in relation to the labor force. Over time this will lead to decreasing benefits from the statutory pension insurance. A more conductive problem concerning old-age poverty is the unemployment in East Germany. Many people show disruptions and gaps in their employment biography. For the old-age income situation this is negative in two ways.

* *Corresponding author:* ifo Institute for Economic Research–Branch Dresden, Einsteinstraße 3, D-01069 Dresden, Germany, Phone: +49 (0351)2647628, e-mail: krenz@ifo.de.

** ifo Institute for Economic Research–Branch Dresden, Einsteinstraße 3, D-01069 Dresden, Germany, Phone: +49 (0351)2647624, e-mail: nagl@ifo.de.

*** ifo Institute for Economic Research–Branch Dresden, Einsteinstraße 3, D-01069 Dresden, Germany, Phone: +49 (0351)2647617, e-mail: ragnitz@ifo.de.

First of all, people do not acquire as much entitlement to the statutory pension as they would if they were working. This is especially a problem for long-term unemployed people. After the labor market legislation reforms of 2003 and 2004, this group earns nearly no pension claims during long-term unemployment periods. Second, people are not able to make sufficient private or occupational provision while unemployed.

So is there a growing risk of old-age poverty in East Germany? We try to answer this question focusing on the German statutory pension insurance. We do this because of two reasons. First, there are no reliable data concerning occupational pension schemes and private retirement arrangements. Second, the benefits from the statutory pension insurance are, and will be in 2020, the most important income source for pensioners. Today the share of income from the statutory pension insurance to the whole old-age income is about 90 percent and will only slightly decrease to 85 percent in 2020.[1] Taken this fact into account, we believe that we do a good approximation of the old-age poverty risk. To detect changes we focus on new pensioners in the years 2004 – 2006 and compare them to new pensioners in 2020 – 2022. This is really important to keep in mind when we are talking about post retirement poverty. The figures presented below display not the situation of all pensioners in 2004 – 2006 and 2020 – 2022. Although we are mainly interested in the situation in East Germany, in addition we calculate the situation for West Germany to find similarities as well as differences.

Our analysis starts with a short description of the German Pension System. Hereby especially the statutory pension insurance is explained. After that, Chapter 3 summarizes demographic facts for East Germany. Most important for our analysis are the findings that the share of people living in a relationship increases with age, and that widows are the second largest group of female retirees. In Chapter 4 we present our methodology and data. We construct a micro-simulation-model and use data from the Institute for Employment Research (IAB) and the German Federal Pension Fund. Subsequently, we present our comparison of the situation of new pensioners in 2004 – 2004 and 2020 – 2022. Hereby we start with our calculation for single households in Chapter 5. While the old-age poverty risk for single females does not change, we find a growing risk for single males. The results for couples in Chapter 6 confirm the trend towards a more tense income situation of elderly people in 2020. In Chapter 7 we show that widows are the best protected group with respect to the statutory pension system. Chapter 8 concludes.

2. The German Pension System

The German Pension System is based on three pillars. The first and most important is the statutory pension system. In 2004 over 90 percent of the old-age income

1 See Deutsche Rentenversicherung BUND (2007).

of new retirees in East Germany was based on the statutory pension. This number will decrease slightly to 85 percent in 2020. The second pillar consists of the companies' pension schemes. This pillar will become more important over time. Its average share of the total old-age income in East Germany will increase from 5 percent (2004) to 10 percent (2020). The third pillar consists of private retirement arrangements. The share of these will also rise from 2 percent (2004) to 5 percent (2020).[2]

Because of missing data of private and occupational pensions we focus in the following analysis on the statutory pension scheme in Germany in order to judge the risk of old-age poverty. The percentages above stress that this approach is well justified.

The German statutory pension system is a pay-as–you-go-pension system. The monthly pension (*MP*) of a retired person is determined by four factors as given in the following equation:

$$MP = TF \cdot PF \cdot PPV \cdot PP\,.$$

The Time Factor (*TF*) depends on the retirement age. At the regular retirement age (we assume 65 years) it is equal to one. With respect to old-age pensions, the Pension Factor (*PF*) is also equal to one. It only deviates at other pension types (e.g., surviving dependant's or disability pension). The Pension Point Value (*PPV*) transfers the Pension Points (*PP*) into an amount of money. It is determined by three factors: a demographic factor, the growth rate of wages, and a factor which takes into account the growth of the contribution rate to the statutory pension insurance. The *PPV* is calculated each year separately for East and West Germany. For our analysis we keep the *PPV* as constant. In the following analysis we put our focus on the *PP*. The Pension Points are, besides some special issues (parenting, military service and education), calculated as the fraction of one's individual income to the average income in West Germany. Because of the lower wage level in East Germany, the individual income is multiplied by a raising factor[3] which takes the different wage levels in both parts of Germany into account. Labor income is subject to social insurance contribution up to the social security contribution ceiling.[4] Besides social secured employment, an individual also acquires *PP* during unemployment. Receiving unemployment benefits (*Arbeitslosengeld I)* an amount of 80 percent of the previous income is taken as calculation basis for the *PP*. During long term unemployment (*Arbeitslosengeld II*) the calculation base is 205 € per month. This is equivalent to about 0.1 *PP* per year.

2 See Deutsche Rentenversicherung BUND (2007).

3 In 2008 the raising factor was 1.1827.

4 € 54,600 (East) and € 64,800 (West) in 2009.

3. Demographic Setup in East Germany

The risk of old-age poverty depends strongly on the family status. Hereby it is most important whether an individual lives alone or is also supported by a partner. So what are the facts for East Germany?

The current age pyramid for East Germany[5] in Figure 1 shows that with growing age less non-widowed people live alone. For people over 65 the share is about 2 percent for men and 8 percent for women. In this age-group 85 percent of the men and 47 percent of the women are married. The low percentage of married women is due to the fact that there are a lot of female widows. 45 percent of all over 65-year-old women are widowed in comparison with only 13 percent of men who are widowed. In the following, these shares are assumed for both cohorts.[6]

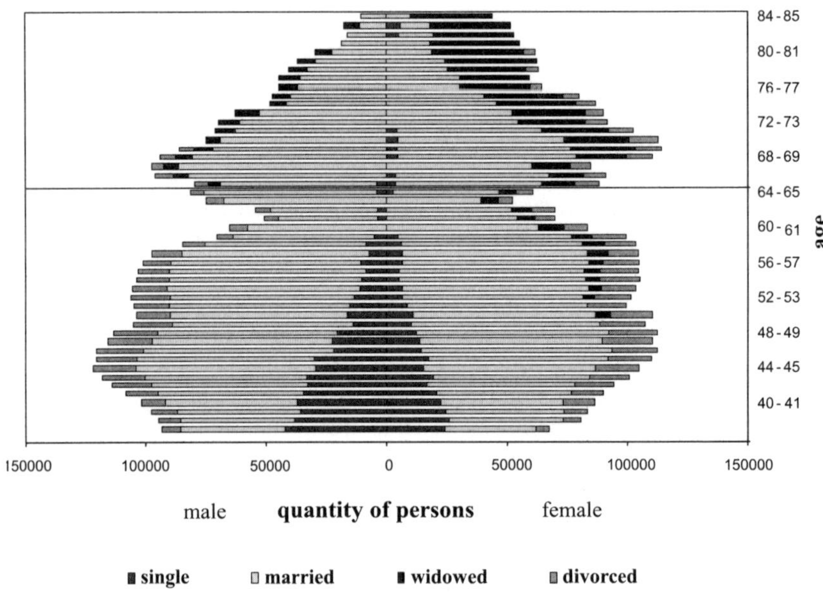

Source: Data from the Federal Statistic Office Germany, Author's calculations.

Figure 1: Family Situation of Households in East Germany

So what are the critical borders for old-age poverty? In the following analysis we define a person or couple as poor if his or their entitlements do not exceed the basic financial security in old-age. For people who live alone, we assume 30 *PP* as

5 The age pyramid was calculated with data from the Federal Office of Statistics.

6 BMFSFJ (2000) shows evidence for higher rates of partnerships for elderly people for different age-groups.

the critical border. 30 *PP* are currently (2008) equivalent to € 700.20 in East Germany and € 796.80 in West Germany. For couples we set 48 *PP* as the critical border. This is currently equivalent to € 1120.32 in East Germany and € 1274.88 in West Germany.

4. Data and Methodology

In contrast to the related literature, we derive Pension Point distributions for elderly single households, couples and widows with respect to education. To identify changes in the risk of old-age poverty, we focus on the number of *PP*s of new pensioners in the period 2004 to 2006 compared to the PPs of people who retire in the period 2020 to 2022. Hereby we distinguish between three skill levels. An individual is considered as low-skilled if he / she is lacking vocational training. A medium-skill level is reached when a vocational training was completed successfully. Individuals with an academic degree are defined as highly qualified. We also draw a separate picture for men and women. We assume for all individuals a retirement age of 65, so the "old" cohort of new pensioners was born between 1939 and 1941. The "young" cohort consists of people who were born between 1955 and 1957. Methodologically our analysis is based on the analysis of elderly single households being explained in Krenz & Nagl (2009).[7]

The most important dataset throughout our analysis is the *IAB-Beschäftigtenstichprobe: Scientific Use File Regionalfile 1975 – 2004 (IABS-R04)* from the German Institute for Labor Market and Job Research (IAB). This academic dataset is a two percent sample of all German workers within the social security system. We choose this dataset mainly because of its size. There are datasets from the Research Center from the German Pension Fund which might fit better due to the information in it, but they are nearly twenty times smaller than the IABS-R04. To carry out such a detailed analysis as intended in our study, we had to choose a really huge dataset. The IABS-R04 provides information on a daily basis from 1975 to 2004 for West Germany and from 1992 to 2004 for East Germany. The IABS-R04 allows to derive PP distributions respectively to age, gender, place of residence and skill. This is possible because the daily income is known, as well as the exact periods of unemployment. The composition of the samples with respect to skills, gender and age in the IABS-R04 is given in Figure 2 and Figure 3.

7 Krenz & Nagl (2009) show the methodology for elderly single households at length as well as a description of the used datasets.

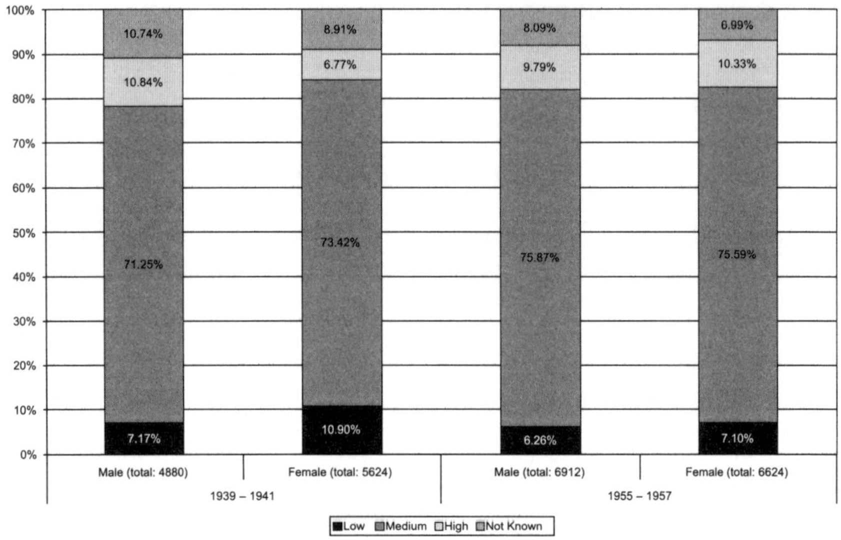

Source: Author's calculations.

Figure 2: Distribution of Skill Levels in East Germany

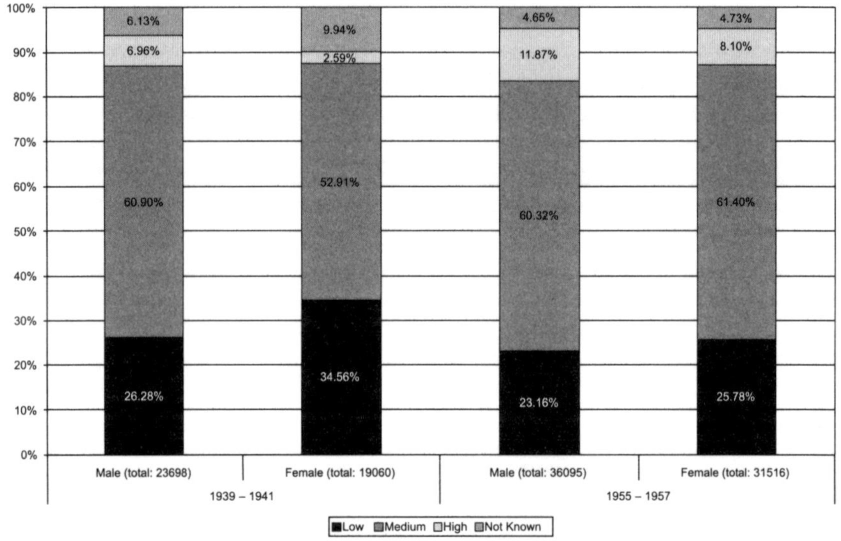

Source: Author's calculations.

Figure 3: Distribution of Skill Levels in West Germany

We drop all persons from the sample which are less then five years in the IABS-R04. We do so because of two reasons. First, we want to exclude civil-servants and self-employed persons. Second an individual has to be reported to the statutory pension insurance for at least five years to achieve a claim.

To derive a picture for the new pensioners in 2020 – 2022 we make projections for individual forthcoming employment patterns. We do this by extrapolation of the employment patterns given in the IABS-R04. We assume that the individual probability of employment, unemployment and long term unemployment will not change until 2020 – 2022.

5. Single-Person Households

Non-widowed single-person households are the group with the highest risk of old-age poverty. As mentioned above, this group is not very large, nevertheless it is a significant part of the society. Because of the lack of specific data, we assume for these households the same gender distribution as for the whole dataset. For males this appears to be an appropriate approach because a full-time working career for men is the regular case independent of family status. For females this is only the case in East Germany. In West Germany, the old-age poverty risk is higher due to low female labor participation.

Males

Figure 4 shows the *PP* distribution of all men in East and West Germany. The dark tone represents the cohort of 1939 to 1941, the bright tone the cohort of 1955 – 1957. Indeed, the mean *PP* level is relatively constant but in both parts of Germany we observe an increasing old-age poverty risk. For single males the risk of old-age poverty rises tremendously in East Germany: whereas in the "old" cohort only 1.34 percent of men acquired less than 30 *PP*, in the "young" cohort this number increases to 31.60 percent.

The special contribution of our analysis is the skill-specific approach. Table 1 describes the rate for persons below the critical value of 30 *PP* with respect to all pensioners of the same skill level. The medium level forms the majority and will be the first to be analyzed in the following. Over time we observe an increasing portion of pensioners below the critical border. Part of this group probably has no or little private or occupational pensions because of their weak income situation. However, some pensioners in this group might be protected by other pensions schemes due to their career type (e.g., civil servant or self-employed). These are people who are insured by the statutory pension insurance for more than five years but skip to civil servant or self-employment later in their career. Deutsche Rentenversicherung Bund (2007) claims that the high percentage of people below 30 *PP*

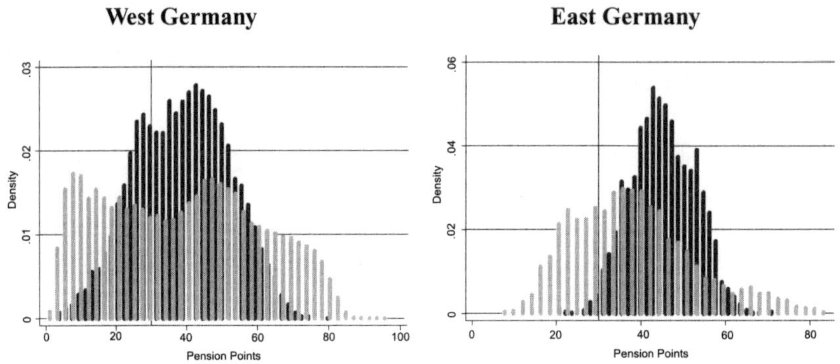

Source: Author's calculations.

Figure 4: Pension-Point-Distribution of Male Pensioners

Table 1

Percentage of Male Pensioners under 30 *PP* with Respect to all Single Males

	West Germany		East Germany	
skill level	1939–41	1955–57	1939–41	1955–57
Medium	21.98%	36.32%	0.93%	31.27%
High	22.62%	30.96%	none	17.52%
Low	45.57%	54.69%	8.19%	67.25%
All	28.26%	39.17%	1.34%	31.60%

Source: Author's calculations.

is caused by this. In general, we can outline that the main part of medium skilled single males in both parts of Germany will get a statutory pension at a sufficient level. In East Germany the statutory pension provides a main part of the whole old-age income, while especially in West Germany private and occupational pensions back up the statutory pension.

The employees with a graduate degree are a case apart, because of two facts. This group contains a great number of people working outside the statutory pension system (civil servants as well as the self-employed) receiving only few pension points. High-skilled employees inside the social security system normally reach a high average level of statutory pension in both regions and for all cohorts and will not face the risk of old-age poverty.

The scenario for employees without vocational education is the most critical. Our forecast for this group shows a high percentage of people near or below the critical *PP* value. Except for the "old" cohort in East Germany a minimum of 45 percent has less than 30 *PP*. Comparing the cohorts, we find that the huge unemployment and the low income reduces the accrued PP of the "younger" cohort dramatically. In times of former GDR this group earned comparable wages to medium-skilled workers. Due to the structural change after German unification labor market chances of low-skilled workers were worsened. But also in West Germany more then 54 percent of the "young" cohort face a high old-age poverty risk. With respect to the fact that many employees of this education level are often not able to acquire private or occupational pensions, a high share of this group needs public basic financial security in old-age (*Grundsicherung im Alter*).

Females

The situation of the females is quite different to the situation of the males. On average, the percentage of women with less than 30 PP is constant at about 51 percent in East Germany.

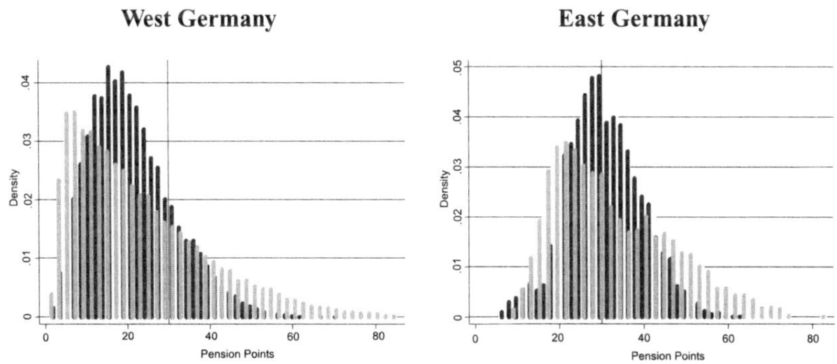

Source: Author's calculations.

Figure 5: Pension-Point-Distribution of Female Pensioners

Table 2

Percentage of Female Pensioners under 30 PP with Respect to all Single Females

	West Germany		East Germany	
skill level	1939–41	1955–57	1939–41	1955–57
Medium	77.31%	70.22%	51.41%	52.25%
High	68.54%	58.34%	7.67%	22.80%
Low	89.80%	84.68%	84.68%	81.35%
All	81.66%	72.64%	51.39%	51.36%

Source: Author's calculations.

The distribution of PP is described in Figure 5 for all women in East and West Germany. Thereby females show a typical right-skewed distribution except for the "old" cohort in East Germany. Again, the mean *PP* level is relatively constant but in both parts of Germany we observe a high old-age poverty risk for all cohorts. In general, the percentages beneath the critical border are lower for East German women.

Medium-skilled women are better protected in East Germany. The reason for this can be found in the employment situation in the former GDR. Females often worked full-time in contrast to females in West Germany, where many women were employed only part-time. We found evidence for this fact in our dataset and it is approved by Deutsche Rentenversicherung Bund (2007). In absence of other protection (e.g., via family) more then 70 percent of both cohorts in West Germany will need social transfers to reach the level of basic financial security. The reason is the traditional choice to be employed part-time or to be a housewife. In West Germany the "young" cohort of medium-skilled women shows a stronger tendency to full-time employment, so some women generate higher levels of PP which leads to a decreasing risk of poverty. There is a different situation in East Germany. The higher labor participation of females here leads to a lower percentage of women which face an old-age poverty risk.

Quite a different picture arises for highly qualified females. Here we find strong differences in both cohorts in East and West Germany. While single women with an academic degree in East Germany reach approximately the mean *PP* level of medium-skilled men, about 60 to 70 percent of women in West Germany will get a *PP* level below the critical border. Thereby the increase of women who choose full-time employment in West Germany plays an important role for the decrease of the risk of old-age poverty (minus 10 percent). For East Germany the risk of old-age poverty is much smaller than in West Germany (only the 23 percent of the "young" cohort are affected). Nevertheless, we observe an increase of the percentage in East Germany. The reason is the same as for high-skilled men (civil service, self-employment), but in addition part-time employment and being a housewife also plays a role.

As with low-skilled males, the worst scenario is found with low-skilled females. Over time we observe a constant high ratio of females facing old-age poverty risk. Thereby the high risk for the "old" cohort in East Germany is surprising, because men of the same skill level and cohort are protected like medium-skilled. The rate in both parts of Germany is always over 80 percent. Most of the low-skilled single females will not benefit from private or occupational pensions and so they need access to additional social transfers.

6. Two-Person Households

The old-age poverty risk of couples is the most important issue to be analyzed because the majority of all elderly people live in a relationship. One of our main results is that couples in East Germany do not face a great old-age poverty risk, although the situation will be more tense in 2020.

Methodically we base our two-person household analysis on the results of Statistisches Bundesamt (2008). This survey uses the *Mikrozensus* 2005 to reach information about the family situation of German households. The analysis has shown that 60 percent of all relationships exist between partners with similar educational levels. In 30 percent of the cases, the man has a higher vocational education and in about 10 percent it is reversed. We assume these percentages to hold for both parts of Germany and adopt them on the skill level groups of our dataset (see Figure 2 and 3). Thereby the case of higher skilled women is excluded, because of technical matters and its minor relevance. For the same reasons we exclude relationships being separated by two skill levels.

As a result we get a relative level of different types of households. Our procedure here is the following. We first match men and women with the same skill level. The rest of the men are matched to females of a lower educational level. The rest of the females are assigned to a man with higher education. An example should illustrate our method and its restrictions.

For instance, we observe 1,000 medium-skilled men and 1,000 medium-skilled women in a cohort. 60 percent of all men and women are combined with partners of equal education. Subsequently, 400 medium-skilled women are left to have a relationship with a high-skilled man. The resulting problem is the low quantity of (for example) 100 high-skilled men. 60 are used for equally educated couples and only 40 are left for a constellation with a medium-skilled woman. So the number of higher skilled men and lower skilled women is always determined by the quantity of the group with fewer members in the dataset.

Figure 6 summarizes the resulting percentages of the possible combinations. The five different household-types we have chosen describe over 90 percent of all constellations. "Others" are excluded cases of higher skilled women and gaps of two education levels.

Using this knowledge about possible skill constellations, we construct a model to describe the household incomes received from the statutory pension insurance. The method to create a detailed picture of the households' statutory pensions is to generate random distributions of income levels for the most important cases. We stochastically combine males and females according to their education level, place of residence and cohort. As a result we get PP distributions for the five main types of households (compare Figure 6). We will begin with the most common combination of medium-skilled men and women.

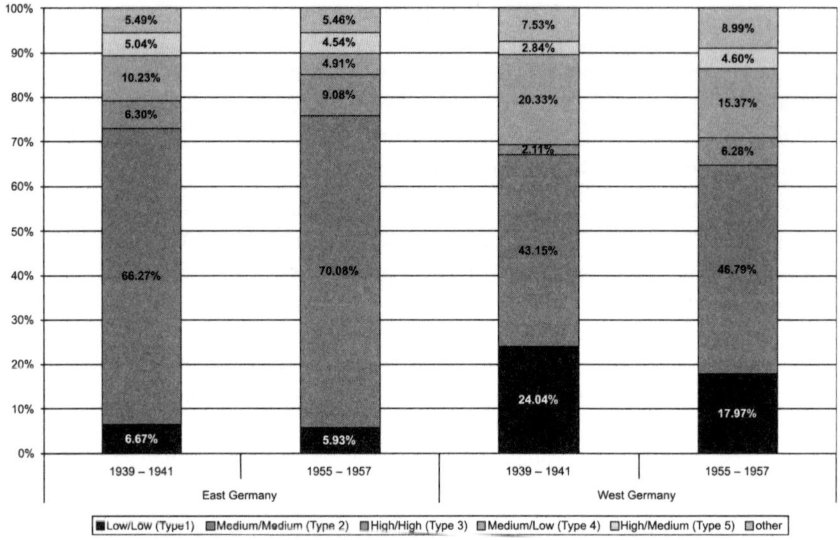

Source: Author's calculations.

Figure 6: Shares of Different Relationships with Respect to all Two-Person Households

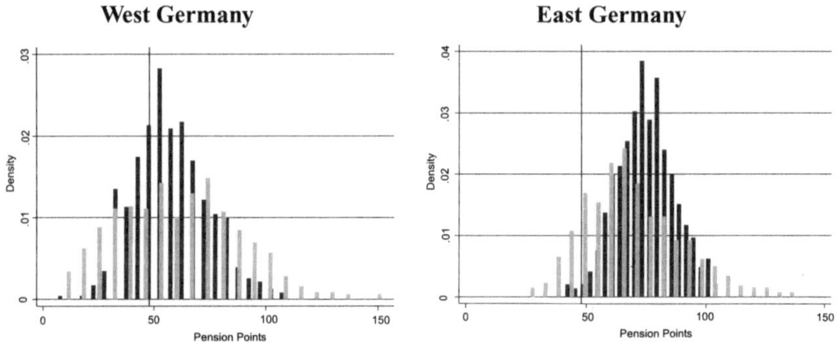

Source: Author's calculations.

Figure 7: Pension-Point-Distribution of Two-Person Households

Table 3

Percentages of Different Relationships under 48 PP with Respect to all Partnerships of this Type

	West Germany		East Germany	
skill levels	1939–41	1955–57	1939–41	1955–57
L / L (type1)	44.99%	54.24%	7.11%	48.23%
M / M (type2)	18.64%	30.09%	0.42%	12.34%
H / H (type 3)	16.19%	21.05%	None	5.01%
M / L (type 4)	24.22%	38.70%	1.35%	22.19%
H / M (type 5)	18.13%	25.55%	None	8.35%
All	28.57%	34.29%	1.27%	12.55%

Source: Author's calculations.

Although the "old" cohort of type 2 households in both parts of Germany faces a relatively low old-age poverty risk (West: 18 percent; East: 0.42 percent) this percentage increases over time. In East Germany the growth is dramatic but the rate is still lower than in West Germany (30 percent vs. 12 percent). Besides increasing unemployment, civil servant status and self-employment induce a growing heterogeneity of incomes. The main part of these age groups seems to be protected against old-age poverty by the statutory pension. This assumption is still even more confirmed if we keep in mind the possibility of additional private and / or occupational pensions, especially in West Germany.

The two following partnership constellations have different importance in both parts of Germany. In East Germany the medium-low-relationship (type 4) takes the second place with a relatively high gap (see Figure 6). In West Germany combination type 1 and 4 shows similar percentages. The main reason for this is the higher percentage of low-skilled people in West Germany.

The situation for medium-low-relationship is similar to the medium-medium households. The old-age poverty risk of the medium-low-relationship, however, is on a higher level. One possible explanation for this may be the bad labor market opportunities of the low-skilled women. In consequence, the situation for such relationships is more problematic than for type 2 households. Especially type 4 households of the "young" cohort face a higher old-age poverty risk (38 percent resp. 22 percent) in both parts of Germany.

As could be expected, the low-low households show the highest old-age poverty risk. Like single low-skilled males only the "old" cohort in East Germany generates a sufficient level of statutory pension (93 percent over 48 *PP*). However, due to the low percentage of low-skilled workers in East Germany the relevance of this combination is rather small. In West Germany this group represents about 20 percent of all two-person households and therefore it increases the risk of old-age poverty. For the "young" cohort in East Germany the same statements as for singles can be made. The risk will increase dramatically (7 percent for the "old" cohort vs. 62 percent for the "young"). In addition to the problem of missing private and / or occupational pension schemes these persons will probably need additional social transfers to reach a basic income security.

The two remaining combinations (type 3 and 5) represent a small number of relationships but for these groups we expect no old-age poverty. We observe about 20 percent of households under the 48 *PP* border. But like in the case of singles, the majority of couples below the critical border is presumably protected outside the statutory pension system (civil service or self-employment). Again the ratio is increasing over time because of heterogeneous labor markets and new career opportunities. Also the possibility of additional private and occupational protection is much higher for these groups (see Deutsche Rentenversicherung Bund 2007).

7. Widows

Widows are the best protected group with respect to the statutory pension system in our analysis. In East Germany widows face no risk of old-age poverty.

For widows we use the results of two-person household analysis with a different critical limit (30 *PP* as for singles). Methodically we assume the household qualification types also for widows. In our analysis we keep the mortality constant over all skill groups. The pension is calculated in a simplified way: A widow gets her own pension and in addition 55 percent of the claim of the deceased partner. Currently there are more specific rules for a dependent's pension. These calculations apply at an income above the old-age poverty level. Therefore this has no impact on our analysis of old-age poverty risk.

In the following we concentrate on widows, because their relevance is much higher than the widowers'. In the group of those over 76 years, widows are the largest group (and growing), while the ratio of widowers is constant over time at a low level. Furthermore, men show a lower old-age poverty risk than women. An additional dependent's pension improves their old-age income situation further.

Table 4

Percentage of Widows Below 30 PP in Respect to all Widows of the Same Type

	West Germany		East Germany	
skill levels	1939–41	1955–57	1939–41	1955–57
type 1 widow (L / L)	49.45%	44.99%	4.74%	31.42%
type 2 widow (M / M)	14.88%	25.78%	0.77%	5.01%
type 3 widow (H / H)	11.21%	16.80%	None	0.90%
type 4 widow (M / L)	21.98%	37.29%	1.13%	14.79%
type 5 widow (H / M)	13.64%	20.21%	None	2.04%
All	27.49%	28.79%	1.27%	5.65%

Source: Author's calculations.

If we compare these percentages to the two-person households we can observe a lower poverty risk for widows of each type. This is because of the fact that the enhancement of the old-age income by the additional dependent's pension often outweighs the loss of the economic advantages of a two person household (economies of scale). Thereby the used poverty limit for two-person households plays an important role.

The groups with the highest risk of old-age poverty are low-skilled widows of medium or low-skilled deceased men (type 1 and 4). The main reason is the low pension claim of the widow which cannot be compensated by the added 55 percent of the deceased partner's pension. In cases of medium-skilled men an additional private and / or occupational pension seems to be more likely as well as life insurance. In contrast type 1 widows face the highest risk of old-age poverty.

In the other cases the percentage of widows with an old-age poverty risk is about or below 20 percent. Also the possibility of additional pension provisions seems to be higher here, especially in cases of high-skilled deceased partners. In East Germany, widows of type 2, 3 and 5 reach a secure level of old-age income by statutory pension. The reason for that is the higher rate of full-time female employees and consecutively the higher level of their own *PP*s. In West Germany the percentages are higher because of the lower pension claims of the widows and the more heterogeneous income structure (see elderly singles).

8. Conclusion

At the beginning we posed the question whether there is a growing risk of old-age poverty in Germany. So what evidence did we find? Comparing the new pensioners in 2004 – 2006 with those of the period 2020 – 2022, we find that in general the risk of post-retirement poverty increases for the latter. With the exception of single females, we observe a growing poverty risk for all household types. The analysis shows also the importance of qualification. Independent from the family status, a higher skill level decreases the poverty risk in old age.

What are the specific findings for East Germany? The poverty risk for single males rises tremendously. Contrary to that, on average the situation of single females seems to be unchanged over time. The situation of couples worsens a little, but is still on a secure level. Widows are the best protected household group in East Germany. They have not and will not have any greater problem in the future.

Is the situation in East Germany worse than in West Germany? Because of the still prevailing employment biographies in the former GDR (with no unemployment), the situation in 2004 – 2006 and in 2020 – 2022 is better in East Germany. In West Germany unemployment began to be an issue in the mid-seventies. This fact is true for nearly every skill level, for every form of household and for men and women.

What are the political implications? First of all, the ongoing political debate about the combination of the two separate pension systems in East and West Germany has nothing to do with the fact of a growing old-age poverty risk, although politicians argue this way. But politicians should be aware of growing old age poverty in the future in both parts of Germany. Second, one has to keep in mind that a reform of the statutory pension system affects the people's retirement situation only in the long term. For people who will retire in ten or fifteen years this has no great effect. Policy makers have to find other ways to protect people against post-retirement poverty.

So what can politics do? One of our main findings is the positive correlation of education and pension benefits. Every measure that improves the education level leads straight forward to lower post retirement poverty. Hereby politics has to accept the challenge to bring as much young people as possible in vocational training and to support their way to a university degree. In addition to this politics have to keep in mind that the current situation at the labor market direct translates into the retirement situation in the future. Consequently one of the main political topics should be the reduction of unemployment. Besides benefits from the statutory pension insurance private retirement arrangements are important to secure oneself against old-age poverty. Hereby politics could perhaps support private and occupational pension arrangements via relief payments or tax incentives.

References

BMFSFJ (2000): "Partnerschaft und Familiengründung – Die Hauptresultate des ersten Ergebnisbandes des Familiensurvey III," Bundesministerium für Familie, Senioren, Frauen und Jugend, Berlin.

Deutsche Rentenversicherung Bund (2007): "Altersvorsorge in Deutschland 2005," Deutsche Rentenversicherung Bund, Berlin.

IABS-R04: IAB-Beschäftigtenstichprobe: Scientific Use File Regionalfile 1975 – 2004, Nürnberg.

Krenz, S. / *Nagl,* W. (2009): "A Fragile Pillar: Statutory Pensions and the Risk of Old-age Poverty in Germany," Ifo Working Paper No. 76.

Statistisches Bundesamt (2008): "Familienland Deutschland, Statistisches Bundesamt," Wiesbaden.

Is There a Growing Risk of Old-Age Poverty in East Germany?

Comment

By Jürgen Schupp*

After nearly 20 years of economic reconstruction in East Germany, the overall income distribution in East and West Germany has narrowed remarkably. Over the 1990s following German reunification, the distribution of real income in East Germany gradually began to resemble that in the West, reflecting a gradual improvement in the overall situation of all private households. Before turning to examine at the phenomenon of (future) old-age poverty, it may be beneficial to briefly take stock of the income development in East and West Germany.

In West Germany, there has been a general increase in income inequality over the past 20 years due to the increasing disparities between lower and higher incomes. In East Germany just after the fall of the Berlin Wall, the income distribution was considerably less unequal than in the West. But starting in the early 1990s there was a rise in inequality in the East, which then slowed and has only begun to increase again in the past few years, although certainly not reaching the higher levels of inequality found in the former West. If one looks at the poverty risk in Germany as a whole (as measured by the European Union's Laeken Indicators), inequality declined in East Germany after reunification as a result of the dramatic increase in income, but has been increasing again steadily since the end of the 1990s. Due to the use of a relative concept of poverty and the measurement of income for Germany as a whole at the point of reunification, the poverty risk rates in East Germany were extremely high and several percentage points higher than those in West Germany.[1] With the significant increase in income throughout the 1990s, poverty rates decreased substantially at first but have increased again in recent years. There has also been a disproportionate increase in poverty risks among the East German population, linked particularly with a strong increase in long-term poverty.

* DIW Berlin, Mohrenstraße 58, 10117 Berlin. E-mail: jschupp@diw.de

1 For details on this rough sketch of income developments, see esp. Jan Goebel, Roland Habich and Peter Krause. Zur Angleichung von Einkommen und Lebensqualität im vereinigten Deutschland. In: *Vierteljahrshefte zur Wirtschaftsforschung,* 78 / 2009, pp. 122 – 145 as well as Markus Grabka and Joachim Frick: Schrumpfende Mittelschicht in Deutschland – Anzeichen einer dauerhaften Polarisierung der verfügbaren Einkommen. In: Wochenbericht des DIW Berlin Heft 10 / 2008, pp. 101 – 108.

In view of this u-shaped evolution of the poverty risk in East Germany, the question that forms the point of departure for the article by Krenz et al. is thus entirely justified. But this leads to yet another question: What role does the phenomenon of old-age poverty play? The German federal government concludes in its 2008 Poverty and Wealth Report[2] that there is currently "no" empirical indication that old-age poverty is a socially significant problem. Furthermore, the German Council of Economic Experts noted in its 2008 report that there has been a steady increase since 2003 in persons aged 65 and older who are entitled to social security in old age, but that at 2.4% of all persons aged 65 and older, their share does not constitute "a particularly worrying finding." At the same time, the Council warns that the "risks of increasing old-age poverty should not be ignored" (SVR 2008, Number 646), and cites the following developments as evidence:

- increased numbers of self-employed persons with below-average incomes, who are probably not adequately insured through the established sectors of the statutory pension system.
- a widening wage gap at the lower end of the distribution, in combination with benefits reductions by the statutory pension insurance.
- increased long-term unemployment and very low pension entitlements accumulated while receiving unemployment benefit II.
- decreased levels of insurance coverage for recipients of invalidity pensions, as well as a lack of possibilities to seek compensation from other sources.

At the same time, in their analysis, the Council does not issue any specific "warning" (SVR 2008, Ziffer 647) regarding the problem of old-age poverty in the East.

In the analysis by Krenz et al., the authors come to a very similar conclusion: namely, that when comparing the same cohorts in East and West Germany, the poverty risk is generally lower in the East due to the more continuous employment biographies there. It is nevertheless useful to briefly recap the central methodological assumptions of the study:

- The projection for cohorts entering retirement between 2020 – 2022 (born 1955 – 1957) and the comparison of persons entering retirement during the period 2004 – 2006 (born 1939 – 1941) are made under the assumption that the individual probabilities of employment, unemployment, and long-term unemployment remain constant; this assumption may be too optimistic given recent developments on the financial market and the global economic crisis.
- A model-based simulation of couple households is conducted with a (proportional) share of educationally homogeneous households, but using educational indicators of very questionable quality derived from data on employees who are subject to compulsory social security contributions.

---

2 Federal Ministry of Labour and Social Affairs: *Der Dritte Armuts- und Reichtumsbericht der Bundesregierung*. Berlin 2008.

- The assumption made in the paper that people will begin receiving their statutory pension benefits at the age of 65 may be too optimistic a scenario, and furthermore, earlier transitions to retirement may be frequent as well, with the attendant reductions in benefits.
- An explicit discussion is missing on how benefit reductions due to reduced earnings capacity following entering retirement are modeled.
- The analysis is limited to the situation of pension entitlements in the statutory pension system and thus completely ignores the potential risk of old-age poverty faced by civil servants and especially self-employed persons.
- The paper completely ignores the effects of the second and third pillars of the statutory pension system as well as those of wealth and assets.
- Due to the use of an "absolute poverty indicator" of less than 30 personal pay points (PP) for singles and less than 48 PP for couples, it would be appropriate to talk not about "poverty" but about "low statutory pension entitlements." After all, whether these legal pension entitlements actually do lead to poverty in the end depends heavily on the scope and level of other possible forms of social security.

Whether the "poverty risk" really will increase in line with the simulation results in the report remains heavily dependent on the assumptions made; the most important shortcoming of the study is its failure to take into account not only all forms of social compensation by the federal government but also possible strategies for private provision.

More convincing findings have been presented in other empirical studies calling attention possible future problems in the income situation of older people in East Germany. One DIW study based on the Socio-Economic Panel (SOEP) data[3] found that the gap in the income distribution expanded between 2002 and 2007 and that this has had a particularly severe impact on the elderly in East Germany due to the Hartz reforms and higher long-term unemployment, entailing that the risk of old-age poverty in East Germany may increase. According to the SOEP analyses, this is especially true of the age cohorts studied by Krenz et al. The price decline in real estate is higher in East Germany and comparatively few East Germans even own homes as a form of investment, and due to the declining pension levels people will have to fall back more and more on private old age provisions and the increasing gap in wealth inequality between East and West Germany could increase the risk of poverty, especially in East Germany.

As a second empirical note, I would like to call attention to recent developments in pension insurance entitlements. Here, we see an increasing percentage of recently retired pensioners with reduced retirement income.[4]

---

3 Frick, Joachim R. and Markus M. Grabka: Gestiegene Vermögensungleichheit in Deutschland. In: *Wochenbericht des DIW Berlin* 76 / 2009, pp. 54 – 67.

- The percentage of reductions among those affected has been increasing considerably since the late 1990s, particularly in the states of the former East.
- Over 60% of recently retired male pensioners and over 70% of recently retired female pensioners living in East Germany were affected by pension reductions in 2007.
- In the former West German states, pension reductions have lowered pension benefits for two in every five recently retired pensioners.
- The increase in pensions subject to pension reductions is due, among other things, to the discontinuation of regulations protecting legitimate expectations, but also reflects specific regional features of labor markets for insured people over 60.

To add a third empirical aspect, I would like to mention the 2005 old-age provision study (AViD) of the German statutory pension system. This study has been used as the basis for projections on the 65th year of life of its youngest target cohort–individuals born between 1957 and 1961.[5] According to the findings of this simulation, eligibility for statutory pension benefits will be considerably reduced for recent cohorts, particularly in East Germany, but the net amount of retirement income will not be reduced to the same degree. According to these findings, single women in the former East in recent cohorts will face a disproportionate risk of having to get by with significantly lower net retirement income.

If one balances these findings against those presented by Krenz et al., one can state that reliable model estimates would only be possible with a comprehensive database covering all three pillars of the German pension insurance system. In addition, poverty analyses require realistic evaluation of the household context as well as balanced consideration of the tax and transfer system. The statutory pension insurance will apparently remain the central element of retirement provisions, especially for people with low income in old age – despite the growing importance of the second and third pillars of the German pension system. Among younger cohorts in East and West, unfavorable employment biographies and reforms reducing the level of pension benefits converge, and both feed into growing inequality in pension payments between the stock of pensioners and new entrance cohorts, increasing the likelihood of increased claims for social benefits. Only for particular groups within the population (people living alone) are there signs of a specifically East German poverty risk.

---

[4] Himmelreicher, Ralf K., and Stuchlik, Andrej: Entwicklung und Verteilung von Entgeltpunkten in der gesetzlichen Rentenversicherung, Deutsche Rentenversicherung 6/2008, pp. 532–545.

[5] Altersvorsorge in Deutschland 2005. Final Report.

Will There Be a Shortage of Skilled Labor? An East German Perspective to 2015

By Herbert S. Buscher,* Eva Dettmann,* Marco Sunder,* and Dirk Trocka*

Abstract

We analyze the supply of and demand for skilled labor in an East German federal state, Thuringia. This state has been facing high unemployment in the course of economic transformation and experiences population ageing and shrinking more rapidly than most West European regions. In a first step, we use extrapolation techniques to forecast labor supply and demand for the period 2009–2015, disaggregated by type of qualification. The analysis does not corroborate the notion of an imminent skilled-labor shortage but provides hints for a tightening labor market for skilled workers. In the second step, we ask firms about their appraisal of future recruitment conditions, and both current and planned strategies in the context of personnel management. The majority of firms plan to expand further education efforts and hire older workers. The study closes with policy recommendations to prevent occupational mismatch.

JEL Classification: J11, J21, J24

Keywords: demographic change, labor demand for high skilled workers, labor force forecast, vocational training

1. Introduction

Human capital is a crucial factor for economic growth in twenty-first-century Europe. As most European countries face the problem of an ageing and shrinking population – and even more so among the labor force – the future trajectory of human capital and the consequences for economic growth have gained considerable attention. While prophecies of skilled-labor shortages have been lessened by the current financial and economic crisis, one may fear nevertheless that such problems could become chronic because demographic changes do not follow the short-run pattern of business cycles. East Germany may provide an interesting ex-

---

* Halle Institute for Economic Research, Kleine Märkerstraße 8, 06108 Halle, Germany. *Corresponding author:* Herbert S. Buscher, Halle Institute for Economic Research, Germany. E-mail address: herbert.buscher@iwh-halle.de.

The authors thank Christian Schmeißer for his excellent support in preparing and analyzing the survey of Thuringian firms. The Thuringian Ministry of Economics, Technology, and Labor provided financial support. Any remaining errors are our own.

ample, inasmuch as the implosion of birth rates following German reunification implies that currently only very small cohorts are reaching working age. At the same time, the economic transformation process, which resulted in soaring unemployment rates, still has ramifications in the present day. We use evidence from the federal state of Thuringia, which reflects the East German experience quite well.

As Figure 1 shows, the number of young adults will drop by more than 40 percent. This process has already started in the group of young people who leave school and apply for apprenticeships. In the cohort aged 20 – 24 years (most of whom have already completed vocational training), the consequences of demographic change will show up in the next years, reaching a trough in 2015. The age composition of the employees is also changing: between 2002 and 2007, the share of employees aged 55 years or older had already increased by nearly two percentage points, whereas the share of employees aged 35 years to 49 years dropped by more than one percentage point. Generally speaking, it will become more difficult for firms to meet their demand for qualified and highly qualified personnel. This might be considered as an additional challenge for the economic development of Thuringia, which has not yet fully reached the West German average.

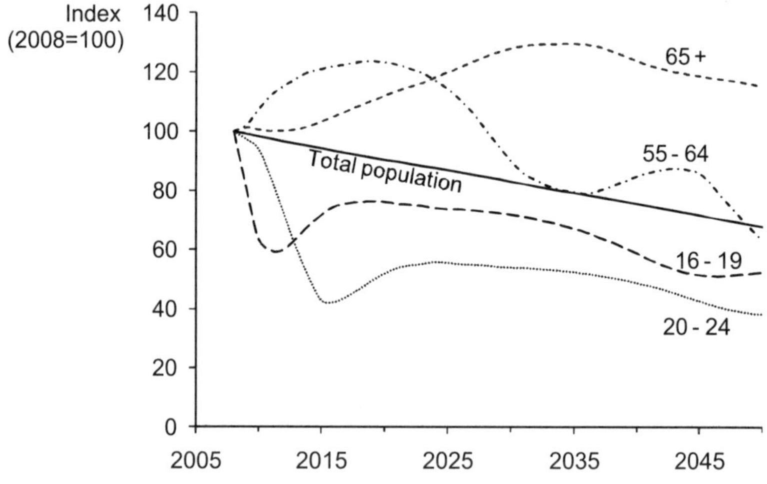

Source: Authors' calculations on the basis of the 11th coordinated population forecast by the German Statistical Office.

Figure 1: Population Forecast for Selected Age Groups in Thuringia

In 2007, GDP per hour worked in Thuringia amounted to 70 percent of the respective West German value, and the unemployment rate of 11.3 percent exceeded the Western level by almost 5 percentage points. Nine out of 10 Thuringian firms employ fewer than 20 workers. Approximately 63 percent of the employees work in the service sector, whereas the sectors industry and construction amount to 33 percent, and agriculture (including mining and power supply) to 4 percent of employment covered by social security. With respect to the occupational structure, metalworking jobs play a major role in Thuringia, and their share among total dependent employment has risen in the last years. Currently, 12 percent of Thuringian employees work in this field of occupation, a figure similar to office jobs. While 27 percent of all employees in Thuringia are older than 50 years, this share amounts to 23 percent in Germany as a whole. Female employment amounts to 48 percent of the employees in Thuringia, compared to 44 percent in West Germany.

On average, workers in the state have a higher (formal) qualification level than their West German counterparts. Due to high unemployment in East Germany, recruiting workers who were overqualified for a certain position used to be common practice. As these workers could also be assigned to higher qualified tasks within the firm, experience of training investment may have been rare until now. A further concern in the context of skilled-labor supply is the high out-migration of young people, especially women, towards West German states, mostly to Bavaria and Hesse (Kubis and Schneider 2007). And in most cases, people leaving Thuringia have at least a medium-level qualification. Commuting to other states remains a frequent phenomenon as well: one in six employees living in Thuringia works outside the state.

Taking these characteristics into account, this article offers evidence on the appraisal of future recruitment problems by small and medium-sized firms, and on their current and planned strategies in the context of personnel management. The article is organized as follows. First we present our forecast results for labor demand and labor supply in Thuringia. A comparison of demand and supply then provides an impression of possible shortages of skilled labor. Next we offer the results of a survey of firms in Thuringia on problems and strategies in the context of personnel management. The study concludes with policy recommendations for the prevention of occupational mismatch.

2. Forecast of Labor Demand and Supply in Thuringia

In order to obtain an impression of possible shortages in the labor market, we forecast the demand and supply of labor in Thuringia for the period 2009–2015. We apply the Manpower Requirement Approach, which allows us to distinguish conditions for several types of qualification (e.g., Blaug 1967). It is commonly applied in the literature for labor market developments, for example in European countries (e.g., Beekman et al. 1991, Bonin et al. 2007) or the OECD (Schömann et al. 2000). After describing the method, and forecasting the development of supply and demand, we juxtapose the qualification-specific results.

Manpower Requirement Approach

This method is characterized by separately forecasting demand and supply. Interactions between both sides of the labor market are not considered, i.e., adjustment and substitution effects due to wages are neglected.

The future volume of labor demand is assumed to follow the development of economic sectors. It is further assumed that growth of a particular sector will lead to proportional rise in the demand for each qualification level. Substitutions between the qualification levels are not considered.[1]

Future Labor Supply

In order to determine the future labor supply, three important aspects have to be considered: demographic developments, the qualification of the population, and their labor market participation. For the forecast of demographic trends, we use the results of the 11th coordinated population projection of the Federal Statistical Office (Statistisches Bundesamt 2006), variant 1.[2] According to this projection, the population in Thuringia will decrease by about 7 percent in the forecasting period. The potential labor supply, the population aged between 15 years and 65 years, is of particular importance for economic development. In this group, the population decline is even stronger. In Thuringia – as in the other East German states – demographic change starts to affect the working-age population in the period considered.

The actual labor supply consists of the persons who want to work, depending on labor market conditions. In our forecast we use the 'labor force' concept, which covers both employed persons and unemployed job seekers, irrespective of their registration at the Federal Employment Agency. While our definition of labor force includes commuters who live in Thuringia and work in a different state, it excludes commuters from other states who work in Thuringia. To predict the share of the labor force among the total population, we consider age-specific labor force participation rates. As the labor force participation varies by qualification level, the qualification of the Thuringian population is considered as well. According to the vocational qualification, the following qualification structure is defined: low-skilled persons have no vocational education degree; skilled persons are indivi-

1 Another strand of forecasting literature uses macroeconomic models to estimate the development of the labor market (Fuchs and Söhnlein 2005, Meyer et al. 2007, Reinberg and Hummel 2002). In these models, assumptions are made about the interdependencies of and relations between single market segments and the behavior of the actors. Then the development of the labor market and the economic sectors is deduced from the results of these assumed interactions. However, it is argued in the literature that such models substitute the uncertainty of labor market development by the uncertainty of the development of exogenous factors and implied interactions (Bonin et al 2007).

2 This variant assumes a nearly constant fertility (1.4 children per woman), a rising life expectancy (88 years for women and 83.5 years for men in 2050), and an annual net immigration of 100,000 persons to Germany.

duals with vocational education and higher job-specific qualifications, such as technician or master craftsman; and high-skilled persons have finished an academic education.

Age-specific information on the current labor force participation rate and the qualification structure can be found in the German Micro Census (Mikrozensus) 2005.[3] From these data, information on the highest vocational qualification for the residents of Thuringia is used to determine the qualification structure. However, there is a problem in determining the qualification of young people aged 15 – 29 years, for they may still attend education institutions and not yet have obtained their final degree. As a remedy, the qualification structure in the age group 30 – 40 years is assigned to individuals aged below 30 years. At ages above 30 years, about three-quarters of the population constitute the skilled group, approximately 15 percent have an academic degree, whereas one in 10 is a member of the low-skilled group.

For each qualification level we determine the age-specific labor force participation rate based on the Micro Census data of 2005. This is again problematic for the group of young adults, because many of them attend school or other education institutions. From the information on the type of the education institution, we draw conclusions about the future qualification level. It is assumed that people attending a vocational school will acquire the corresponding level of qualification (vocational education). Similarly, students at colleges and universities are regarded as high-skilled persons (academic education). For people in general and secondary schooling, the qualification structure of the older Thuringians, between 30 years and 40 years, is again presumed. To determine the labor force participation rate of young adults, we assume that people currently attending any kind of education are not part of the labor force. The resulting age- and qualification-specific labor force participation rate is presented in Figure 2.

Almost 80 percent of the 20-year-old low-skilled persons are already part of the labor force. Until the age of 50 years, labor market participation fluctuates between 80 percent and 90 percent, strongly decreasing in the following years to 10 percent by age 63. Among the skilled persons group, the participation rate of the 25-year-olds is about 80 per cent and this increases in the following 10 years of age. At age 35 – 50 years, the labor market participation rate is around 95 percent and declines for older persons, similar to that of the low skilled. Among those with higher education, the labor force participation is only around 20 percent, even at age 65. At the age of 25 years the participation rate amounts to only about 10 percent, among the 30-year-olds to approximately 60 percent, and it increases in the following three years of age to over 90 percent. This development reflects the much longer

[3] The Micro Census is a survey of socio-economic conditions in Germany, conducted by the Federal Statistical Office. The scientific use file employed in the present study covers approximately 0.7 percent of the population. URL: http: // www.forschungsdatenzentrum.de / bestand / mikrozensus / index.asp.

period of education in this group. Among high-skilled people between 30 years and 60 years of age, the labor force participation rate is about 95 percent.

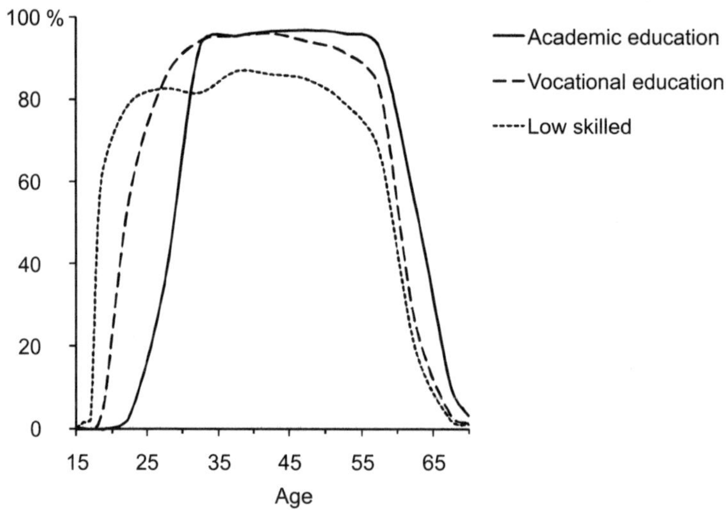

Source: Authors' calculations on the basis of German Micro Census 2005.

Figure 2: Qualification-Specific Labor Force Participation Rate of the Thuringian Population in 2005 (Smoothed)

To complete the labor supply forecast, we combine the projection of the total population with our estimates for the qualification structure and the age- and qualification-specific participation rates. In doing so, we assume that the currently observed qualification structure and the labor force participation will not change in the forecast period.

Under these assumptions, a decline in total labor supply from approximately 1.153 million persons in 2009 to approximately 1.045 million in 2015 is expected. This development is largely driven by the decreasing supply of skilled persons. By 2015, the number of persons at this skill level reduces by approximately 88,000 to a level of 800,000 persons. This is a reduction of about 10 percent. The number of the high skilled reduces to a much lesser extent: 10,000 persons or 6 percent. In 2015, a labor supply of about 160,000 high-skilled persons is expected in Thuringia. The number of low-skilled persons decreases by about 10,000 – or 11 percent – to a level of approximately 90,000 persons in 2015. Whether this development implies a future "bottleneck" at the labor market, however, depends on the development of labor demand.

Future Labor Demand

Two factors influence the amount and the structure of desired recruitment in the future.[4] First, the replacement demand, i.e., the demand due to the retirement of older employees, has to be considered. Secondly, the so-called expansion demand induced by structural changes, technical progress, and economic growth influences the number of employees required in the future. We assume that changes in sector structure of the Thuringian economy translate into changes in labor demand by professions, which can ultimately be associated with the three types of qualification considered above.

The first step is to identify the purely age-related replacement demand under status quo conditions, i.e., without taking structural changes into account. We determine the replacement demand on the basis of information provided by the Federal Employment Office (Bundesagentur für Arbeit) on the age structure of Thuringian employees in jobs covered by social security in 2007.[5] Every year, compensation for retired employees is necessary. In the forecast period from 2009 to 2015, this is the case for all employees at the age of 55 – 63 years in 2007. The following considerations lead to the identification of this age group: The legal retirement age in 2007 is 65 years.[6] According to information from the German Pension Fund (Deutsche Rentenversicherung) the actual retirement age in East Germany, however, is 63 years on average. Assuming that this retirement age remains constant during the forecast period, the replacement demand for the year 2009 contains all employees between 63 years and 65 years of age.[7] For subsequent years, we assume that all retirement occurs at age 63. Overall, we expect an age-related replacement demand of approximately 89,000 in the 46 occupations considered (Table 1, column 1).[8]

In the second step, we assess the influence of structural changes, technical progress, and economic growth on future labor demand. In order to capture their impact, past growth rates of employment in the period 2003 – 2007 within each of eight economic sectors are extrapolated.[9] Thus, changes in the relative importance

4 We abstract away from recruitment due to labor turnover prior to retirement age as our forecast is tailored to the macro-level.

5 Using figures for currently employed persons as the basis for prediction of the future labor demand implies the assumption of no labor shortage at present. The Bundesagentur für Arbeit provided us the relevant data.

6 The government decision to increase the retirement age to 67 years is implemented stepwise from 2012 to 2029 and is therefore negligible for the present forecast.

7 To determine the number of employed older persons, the age-specific participation rates of 2007 are extrapolated to 2009.

8 In this application, the original occupation classification system of the Federal Employment Office is condensed into 46 categories.

9 We consider the following sectors: agriculture, forestry, fishing; mining, energy, water supply; manufacturing; construction; trade, hospitality, transportation; finance, industry related services; public administration; public / private services.

of different sectors and the associated development of sector-specific labor demand are the basis for the projection of the expansion demand. In the forecast period, considerable shifts in the sector structure of the Thuringian economy are projected. The importance of the primary sector as well as the building & construction sector will further decline, while the tertiary sector becomes more relevant. For the manufacturing sector, too, an increasing number of employees is expected.

Assuming an invariant occupation structure within the sectors, the change-induced expansion demand by occupation can be determined. Overall, we expect a negative expansion demand of approximately 10,000 employees until the end of the forecast period. Summarizing the occupation-specific information on the previously identified replacement demand and the expansion demand yields the figure for "net desired recruitment." In the forecast period, this figure amounts to approximately 80,000 persons. Table 1 presents the occupation-specific net desired recruitment as well as its constituent elements, replacement and expansion demand. Additionally, the table contains information on the net desired recruitment related to the stock of employees in 2007.

As one might have expected, the figures show large differences in the absolute amount of future demand among the occupation categories considered. Altogether, net desired recruitment is largely driven by age-related replacement demand. Related to the stock of employees in 2007, the demand concentrates on occupations with a large proportion of high-skilled employees, mainly in technical and engineering occupations as well as in the service sector.

Labor demand is assumed to be unaffected by worker replacement requirements, so that changes in the stock of employees required can result only from expansion demand. In order to juxtapose qualification-specific labor demand and supply, we now concentrate on the three-category qualification scheme and the associated expansion demand. From the occupation-specific forecast of the expansion demand we can derive the development of future demand in the three levels of qualification. We assume that occupation-specific changes of the expansion demand will lead to proportional changes in the demand for each qualification level. In other words, the qualification structure within occupations is regarded as constant.

Labor demand will decrease in every one of the three qualification levels. In 2015, the demand for high-skilled and skilled workers is approximately 1 percent and 1.5 percent lower than at the beginning of the forecast period, amounting to approximately 81,000 and 555,000 persons respectively. The reduction in demand for low-skilled persons is about 0.7 percent in the forecast period – to 75,000 persons in 2015.

Future Labor Shortage in Thuringia?

When comparing the forecasts of demand and supply, one should keep in mind that the underlying data originate from data sources that apply different definitions of employment. The forecast of labor demand is based on information from the

Table 1

Occupation-Specific Future Labor Demand in Thuringia, 2009 – 2015

Occupation category	Replacement demand	Expansion demand	Net desired recruitment	
	(1000 persons)	(1000 persons)	(1000 persons*)	related to stock 2007 (percent)
Bankers, insurance sales agents	1.1	2.8	3.9	34.4
Protective service workers	2.7	0.7	3.4	30.8
Waste management and cleaning workers	2.8	1.6	4.3	26.3
Teachers	6.2	–1.3	4.9	25.7
Chemists, physicists, mathematicians	0.2	0.1	0.3	25.0
Managers, accountants	2.6	0.7	3.3	24.7
Engineers	2.5	0.8	3.3	24.3
Lawyers, judges, and related occupations	0.1	0.1	0.1	22.0
Physical technicians	0.6	0.4	1.0	20.8
Laborers	2.2	3.1	5.3	20.6
Engineering technicians	3.0	0.3	3.3	17.2
Journalists, translators, librarians, archivists	0.5	-0.1	0.4	17.0
Ministers, representatives, administrators	1.8	-0.5	1.4	17.0
Financial clerks, data processing specialists	2.2	0.6	2.8	16.6
Textile and clothing workers	0.6	0.1	0.7	15.2
Dispatching service workers	1.2	0.4	1.5	15.1
Chemical and plastics workers	1.1	0.4	1.6	14.3
Religious workers	0.1	0.0	0.0	13.8
Printing workers	0.2	0.1	0.3	13.3
Stock clerks, warehouse workers	2.3	0.2	2.5	13.1
Paper manufacturing and processing workers	0.2	0.1	0.3	13.0
Woodworkers	0.2	0.1	0.3	13.0
Housekeeping workers	0.5	–0.1	0.4	12.9
Stonemasons, glaziers, potters, and related occupations	0.5	0.2	0.7	12.7
Miscellaneous sales representatives, and related occupations	0.6	0.2	0.7	12.3
Social and natural scientists	0.2	0.1	0.3	12.0
Administrative support workers	13.0	–2.0	11.1	12.0
Metalworkers, mechanics, installers, toolmakers, and related occupations	8.4	1.3	9.6	11.4
Mining and extraction workers	0.1	0.0	0.1	10.5
Artists, designers, photographers, and related occupations	0.4	–0.1	0.3	9.9
Transportation workers	4.0	–1.2	2.8	9.1
Machine operators and related occupations	1.0	–0.3	0.7	9.0

Continued next page

Table 1 Continued

Occupation category	Replacement demand	Expansion demand	Net desired recruitment	
	(1000 persons)	(1000 persons)	(1000 persons*)	related to stock 2007 (percent)
Food processing workers	1.9	–0.3	1.6	7.6
Social service workers and specialists	4.7	–2.6	2.1	6.5
Merchants and related occupations	5.1	–1.7	3.4	6.3
Electricians, service technicians	2.0	–0.8	1.2	6.0
Communications operators	0.3	–0.1	0.2	5.2
Miscellaneous workers	0.5	–0.2	0.3	3.3
Agricultural and forest workers	2.6	–2.1	0.5	2.5
Furnishings workers	0.1	–0.1	0.0	1.6
Restaurant and hotel keepers, waiters, and related occupations	0.6	–0.5	0.1	1.4
Healthcare practitioners and supporters	4.6	–3.9	0.7	1.4
Cabinet and model makers	0.3	–0.3	0.1	1.1
Hair cutters, beauticians	0.5	–0.4	0.0	0.4
Painters and related occupations	0.5	–0.6	–0.1	–2.0
Construction workers	2.3	–4.6	–2.3	–7.6
Overall	89.0	–9.5	79.6	11.0

Note: * Rounding differences may apply.

Source: Authors' calculations based on Employment Statistics of the Federal Employment Office.

Federal Employment Office on employees in jobs covered by social security in Thuringia. This is a rather narrow definition of employment. It excludes civil servants, self-employed persons, workers in family businesses, persons in marginal part-time employment, and soldiers. The forecast supply, in contrast, applies the conventional definition of labor force and uses data taken from the German Micro Census for Thuringia, covering all employed persons and unemployed job seekers.

Due to the differing definitions of "labor" in these forecasts, the resulting absolute figures are not directly comparable. However, it is possible to compare the expected changes in labor demand and supply by type of qualification (Figure 3). In the forecast period a reduction of the labor supply as well as the labor demand is expected. Due to the stronger decrease in labor supply, a trend towards a labor shortage in Thuringia is identified. Considering that labor supply includes unemployed job seekers, and unemployment is high, a quantitative labor shortage is not expected in either qualification level until the end of the forecast period.

A comparison between the qualification levels might lead to the conclusion that the relative labor market position of low-skilled employees will improve in the future. However, this group has by far the highest unemployment rate. Instead, the gap in the growth rates for the numerically largest group, skilled labor, must be considered as the most serious challenge for the economy of Thuringia.

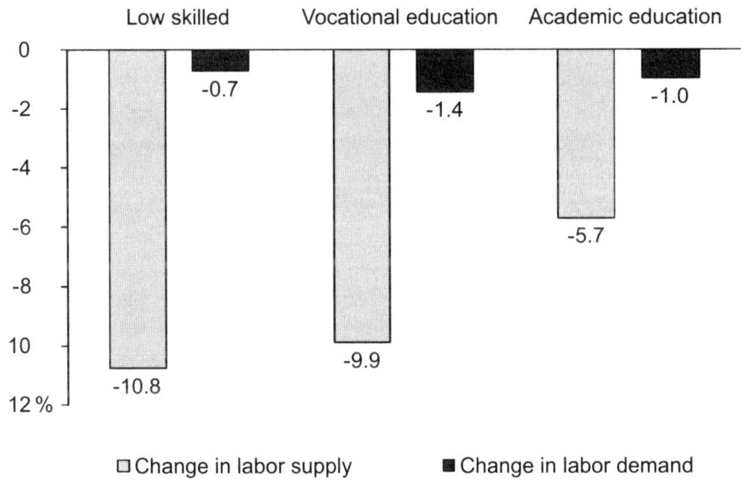

Source: Authors' calculations on the basis of Employment Statistics of the Federal Employment Office and German Micro Census 2005.

Figure 3: Forecast of the Development of Qualification-Specific Labor Demand and Supply in Thuringia, 2009 – 2015, Growth Rates in Percent

3. The Perspective of Firms

We switch the perspective from the 'objective' analysis based on official statistics to the (subjective) perceptions of firms regarding current and future recruitment problems.

Hitherto Observed Problems

Against the backdrop of very favorable business conditions in previous years, one might expect that firms experienced difficulties in hiring skilled workers in Germany as a whole. The intensity of such a bottleneck may not be homogenous across regions in the case of imperfect labor mobility. Considering the high unemployment rates following the economic transformation of the 1990s, it is not obvious that skilled-labor shortages existed in the East German federal states, particularly in Thuringia, in the recent past. A common procedure in the literature is to assemble indicators from aggregated register data (Veneri 1999). However, there is no clear-cut criterion for labor shortages in such an approach, and usually vacancies are difficult to measure as not all of them are necessarily reported to labor offices. In contrast, we resort to two sources of disaggregated data at the level of firms or establishments: the *IAB establishment panel* and a survey of firms in Thuringia conducted by IWH in 2008 (Bellmann 1997, Buscher et al. 2008).

The *IAB establishment panel* is a representative, annual survey of establishments in Germany covering all industry sectors.[10] The 2007 wave places special emphasis on recruitment of skilled workers. In addition to the number of skilled employees hired in the first half of 2007, the data contain the number of positions for skilled workers that could not be filled in the same period. We define the "gross desired recruitment intensity" as the sum of these two components per 1,000 employed skilled workers.[11] Compared to the previous discussion of business expansion and retirement as reasons for net desired recruitment, labor turnover prior to retirement age would constitute an additional motif for firms' recruitment demands. A regional comparison shows that the total recruitment intensity in Thuringia (68 per 1,000 skilled employees within six months) is similar to the respective value for East Germany as a whole, and exceeds the West German level by more than a quarter (Figure 4). Within Thuringia, firms in agriculture / mining and the building sector had above-average recruitment intensity, whereas in West Germany the service sector played a pivotal role. Breaking down the recruitment intensity amount reveals that 11 vacancies per 1,000 skilled employees could not be filled in both East and West Germany, with a somewhat lower figure for Thuringia. The share of filled vacancies is somewhat higher in Thuringia (88 percent) than in East Germany as a whole (84 percent) or West Germany (80 percent). This suggests that firms in Thuringia have faced fewer problems than average in finding skilled personnel in the recent past. However, this observation cannot necessarily be carried over into the future, as the demographic change affects Thuringia more rapidly than West Germany.

Personnel Management Policies in the Context of Expected Problems

In order to investigate expected hiring problems and potential countermeasures by firms with a longer time horizon, we use data from the IWH survey on firms in Thuringia. Interviews covering approx. 1,000 firms were conducted with human resource managers or CEOs in June and July 2008. The survey was designed to cover the most important industry branches of the state; these industries comprise about two-thirds of total employment. Company names were sampled from the Markus database of Creditreform stratified by industry branch and three size classes.[12] The questionnaire covers current personnel policies, training activities (apprenticeships, further education), expectations about changes in the size of the firm's staff, problems in recruiting workers, and planned expansion of programs in the context of personnel management (Table 2).

---

10 URL: http://www.iab.de/en/erhebungen/iab-betriebspanel.aspx/.

11 As the stock of skilled employees is not available for the beginning of the period considered, we use the June 2007 value instead.

12 URL: http://www.creditreform.de/Deutsch/Creditreform/FAQ/Direktmarketing/Firmenprofile_MARKUS.

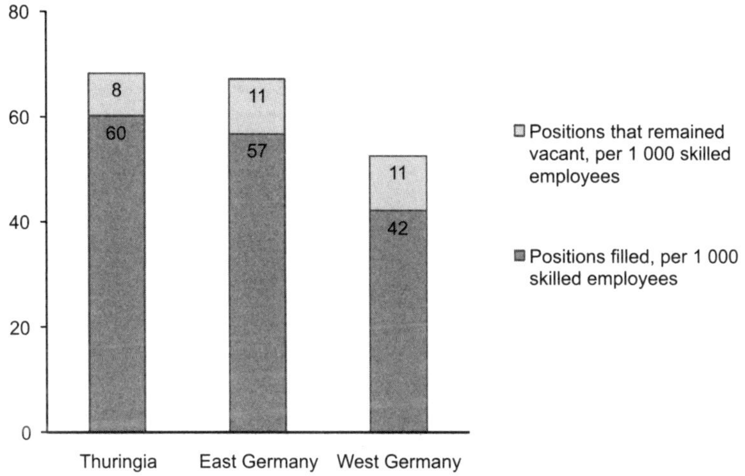

Source: Authors' calculations on the basis of IAB establishment panel 2007.

Figure 4: Gross Desired Recruitment Intensity, January – June 2007

Table 2

Composition of the Regression Sample (n = 944)

Variable	Mean	Variable	Mean
Problems expected when hiring workers?	0.61	Industry: Food production	0.09
Share of workers aged 55+	0.14	Metal production and processing	0.15
Employment outlook: decreasing	0.10	Electrical / precision engineering,	
stable	0.49	optical industry	0.12
increasing	0.41	Commerce and repairing	0.13
Share of workers with college education	0.18	Transport and communication	0.12
Share of master craftsmen	0.07	Business services, real estate, leasing	0.14
Current vacancies?	0.34	Health and social services	0.12
Crafts company?	0.41	Mechanical engineering	0.10
		Miscellaneous industries	0.03

Source: IWH survey on firms in Thuringia, 2008.

We are interested in the association between these management policies and company characteristics, especially the expected incidence of problems in hiring workers in the future. Our "problems" variable is a binary response to the following question: "do you expect problems finding adequate applicants for vacancies within the next five years?" No less than 61 percent of the interviewed firms answered in the affirmative. In order to ascertain whether the perception of problems varies by company characteristics, we estimate a probit regression model. We consider the following company characteristics–which will also be used in consecutive regression equations:

- employment structure (number of workers, age, share of highly qualified staff),
- employment dynamics (current vacancies, five-year outlook),
- type of business (sector, crafts).

We expect that larger firms are more likely to run into problems because of a higher labor turnover and therefore more frequent hiring processes. Similarly, firms with older employees may have higher replacement incentives, and those with greater human capital intensity may face greater difficulties when replacing highly qualified workers if this group is in short supply and cannot be trained within the firm. We define proxies for age structure as the share of workers aged at least 55 years, and for human capital intensity as the share of workers with college education or a master craftsman degree. Furthermore, firms that plan to expand their workforce or already have vacant positions may have a greater probability of experiencing problems. Based on the previous argument of this study, one might also expect differences across the industry spectrum.

The regression results do not support all of our hypotheses (Table 3, column 1). However, current vacancies have a strong effect, with the expected sign: the estimated coefficient of 0.77 translates into a 27 percentage point difference of anticipating problems (at the mean of all other variables). Industry categories, too, affect the expectation of problems, with particularly high rates in mechanical engineering and the metal production industry, which corroborates our occupation-level forecasts of (relative) net desired recruitment. We do not find evidence for elevated problem awareness among crafts companies, though. The impact of employment level is modest: starting from the sample average of the logarithm of employees and averages for other variables, 10 further employees increase the probability of anticipating problems by 1.5 percentage points.

Awareness of problems in the near future may affect the willingness to implement certain personnel management programs tailored to secure the firm's human capital base. We first consider whether three programs are already in progress at the time of the survey: training of apprentice(s), further training, and fringe benefits. About half of the firms in our sample currently have at least one apprentice or pay fringe benefits, while three-quarters conduct further training measures on a regular basis (Table 3, columns 2 – 4). While expected problems seem to be unrelated to training efforts, there is a strong association between expected problems and the payment of fringe benefits, with a marginal effect of 12 percentage points. Considering the composition of the workforce, we find that firms with a higher share of older workers are less tempted to offer perks. A large share of employees with college education predicts a lower probability of training apprentices and higher probabilities of regular further education programs and of fringe benefit payments. Positive employment outlook affects perks only, with marginal effects of

Table 3

Binary Probit Model Coefficients on Expected Problems and (Selected) Implemented Personnel Management Policies

	Problems expected	Implemented personnel management policies		
		Apprenticeship	Further training	Fringe benefits
Problems expected				
Yes		0.09	0.04	0.30***
No		*ref.*	*ref.*	ref.
Share of workers aged 55+	–0.30	–0.52	0.01	–0.45*
Employment outlook:				
decreasing	–0.21	0.21	0.17	0.00
stable	*ref.*	*ref.*	*ref.*	*ref.*
increasing	0.15	–0.17	–0.05	0.39***
Share of workers with college education	0.08	–0.60***	0.95***	0.36*
Share of master craftsmen	0.08	0.42	0.38	–0.30
Current vacancies? Yes	0.77***	–0.03	0.17	0.35***
No	*ref.*	*ref.*	*ref.*	*ref.*
Number of employees (*natural log.*)	0.08**	0.68***	0.14***	0.08**
Industry:				
Food production	–0.70***	–0.13	0.04	0.33*
Metal production and processing	–0.15	0.19	0.16	0.04
Electrical / precision engineering, optical industry	–0.59***	–0.24	0.39**	0.31*
Commerce and repairing	–0.59***	–0.10	0.52***	0.17
Transport and communication	–0.25	–1.00***	0.26	0.31
Business services, real estate, leasing	–0.55***	–0.43**	0.48**	0.11
Health and social services	–0.26	–0.69***	1.52***	0.15
Mechanical engineering	*ref.*	*ref.*	*ref.*	*ref.*
Miscellaneous industries	–0.35	–0.04	0.91***	0.03
Crafts company?				
Yes	–0.02	0.15	–0.05	–0.03
No	*ref.*	*ref.*	*ref.*	*ref.*
Intercept	0.20	–1.57***	–0.31	–0.76***
n	944	944	931	932
Pseudo-R^2	0.115	0.309	0.094	0.078

Notes: *** / ** / * indicate statistical significance at the 1 percent / 5 percent / 10 percent levels respectively, based on heteroscedasticity-robust standard errors.

Source: IWH survey on firms in Thuringia, 2008.

+16 and +14 percentage points for planned expansion of employment and at least one currently vacant position, respectively. While metal-producing and mechanical engineering firms have a particularly high tendency to invest in training apprentices, the health sector has the highest probability of regular further training activities, which may be related to legal requirements in this field. No clear pattern emerges for fringe benefits. We also find no meaningful differences across the implemented personnel management policies under consideration between crafts companies and the remaining firms.

We now turn to programs that firms planned to implement or expand within the five years following the survey. Figure 5 plots the sample frequencies regarding 10 selected measures that might prove useful in recruiting workers (apprenticeship, internship, job fairs, cooperative tertiary education, hire from abroad, hire of older workers), increasing employee loyalty (further training, employment of workers beyond retirement age, part-time jobs), or downsizing labor demand. The bars indicate the percentage of firms that plan either to introduce such measures or to expand their efforts in these fields. The most frequently quoted strategies refer to further training and hiring of older workers. These two measures appear to be a sensible response to the imminent demographic changes in labor supply. Again, we estimate binary probit models to unveil the present determinants of future personnel management strategies (Table 4). The probability of conducting such plans is, in most cases, positively associated with firm size and the expectation of problems. The prospect of an increase in labor demand predicts a higher probability of introducing or expanding six of the measures considered. While crafts companies do not differ from other firms in most cases, they are less inclined to hire older workers for their workshops.

The fact that more than half of the firms in the industries considered express the fear that they will have problems in filling vacant positions in the near future could be a sign of a tightening labor market for skilled workers.[13] While many of the firms anticipating such problems have already planned reaction strategies to absorb the changes in the demographic composition, some firms may not yet be aware of their future challenges. The strategies cited here all belong to the sphere of the firms. However, they could also be supported or complemented by government action, chambers of commerce, and similar organizations, and we conclude by making some final recommendations for policies to address these issues.

4. Policy Recommendations and Conclusions

We present our policy recommendations for an array of key actors involved in he design of institutional settings of the local labor market. The suggested mea-

[13] Obviously it would be desirable to have comparative figures not only for other regions but also for earlier time periods within Thuringia in order to quantify the magnitude of this trend.

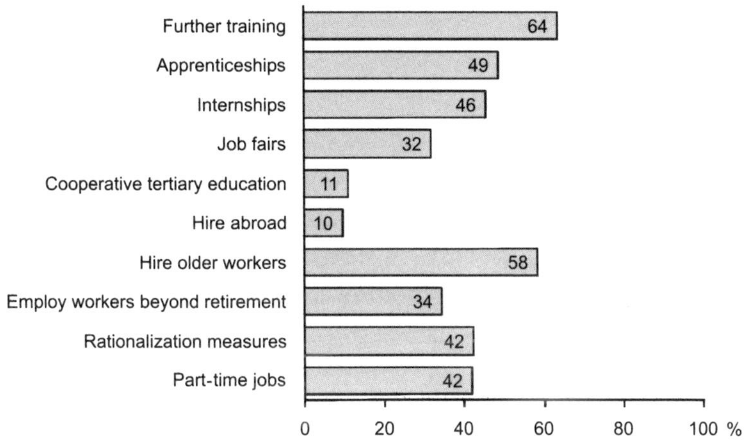

Remark: Multiple responses possible.

Source: IWH survey on firms in Thuringia, 2008.

Figure 5: Percentage of Companies with Planned Expansion of Programs in the Context of Personnel Management

sures have been devised to help maintain the competitiveness of the Thuringian economy and foster economic growth. While currently a shortage of qualified workers is not a pressing issue, the present situation is unlikely to be sustainable in the light of population ageing. As our survey suggests, many firms anticipate problems related to hiring skilled workers in the near future, and seek to implement appropriate countermeasures. The short time-frame available to policy making at the different institutional levels needs to be used efficiently if measures are to be set up to alleviate the problem of shortages in skilled labor in the future.

We group our policy recommendations in three categories: the first category can be headed as "activating existing potentials in the labor market"; the second one has a medium-term horizon and relates to "education and vocational training programs"; and the third category is basically an "information and consulting strategy", directed at firms as well as employees and young people deciding about their future careers. It is useful that the key-actors cooperate and coordinate their behavior, and a combination of the strategies may provide better outcomes than an isolated strategy.

On average, Thuringian employees are older than those in Germany as a whole. This indicates a risk for firms continuing their business in the coming years, as it implies higher replacement demand when at the same time the number of young people entering the labor market drops significantly. This situation calls for the activation of three important human-capital resources for Thuringia: first, there is a large number of commuters who live in Thuringia and work in neighboring states.

Table 4: **Binary Probit Model Coefficients on Planned Expansion of Programs in the Context of Personnel Management**

	Further training	Appren-ticeships	Intern-ships	Job fairs	Coopera-tive tertiary education	Hire abroad	Hire older workers	Employ workers beyond retirement	Rationa-lization measures	Part-time jobs
Problems expected?										
Yes	0.29***	0.21**	0.25***	0.22**	0.29**	0.20	0.46***	0.27***	0.07	0.22**
No	*ref.*	*ref.*	*ref.*	*ref.*	*ref.*	*ref.*	*ref.*	*ref.*	*ref.*	*ref.*
Share of workers aged 55+	–0.57**	–0.31	0.00	–0.24	–0.26	0.60*	0.24	0.97***	–0.16	–0.17
Employment outlook:										
decreasing	–0.04	–0.08	–0.27*	–0.23	0.43*	0.33	–0.16	–0.15	0.37**	0.24
stable	*ref.*	*ref.*	*ref.*	*ref.*	*ref.*	*ref.*	*ref.*	*ref.*	*ref.*	*ref.*
increasing	0.14	0.31***	0.23**	0.24**	0.39***	0.19	0.28***	0.22**	0.03	0.11
Share of workers with college education	0.03	–0.61***	0.38**	0.89***	1.05***	0.75***	–0.24	–0.14	–0.05	–0.02
Share of master craftsmen	0.20	0.20	0.52	0.14	0.22	0.02	0.33	0.48	–0.08	0.24
Current vacancies?										
Yes	–0.08	–0.05	–0.02	0.06	–0.01	0.75***	0.19*	0.09	0.01	–0.20**
No	*ref.*	*ref.*	*ref.*	*ref.*	*ref.*	*ref.*	*ref.*	*ref.*	*ref.*	*ref.*
Number of employees (*natural log.*)	0.21***	0.16***	0.20***	0.34***	0.32***	0.10*	0.08**	–0.02	0.21***	0.11***

Continued next page

Table 4 Continued

Industry:										
Food production	0.15	0.25	–0.10	0.25	–0.67**	–1.07**	0.15	–0.12	0.29	0.58***
Metal production and processing	0.07	0.35**	0.11	0.16	–0.11	–0.03	0.02	0.07	0.23	0.41**
Electrical / precision engineering, optical industry	0.39**	0.37**	0.16	0.22	–0.17	–0.17	–0.04	0.04	0.13	0.56***
Commerce and repairing	–0.09	–0.15	–0.20	0.23	–0.42	–0.20	–0.02	–0.07	–0.35*	0.54***
Transport and communication	–0.17	–0.36*	–0.17	–0.06	–0.55*	–0.24	0.37*	0.32*	–0.12	0.57***
Business services, real estate, leasing	–0.12	–0.06	–0.17	–0.23	–0.38	–0.06	–0.02	0.14	–0.16	0.58***
Health and social services	0.37*	0.06	0.09	0.13	–0.42*	–0.01	–0.16	0.11	–0.11	0.85***
Mechanical engineering	*ref.*	*ref.*	*ref.*	*ref.*	*ref.*	*ref.*	*ref.*	*ref.*	*ref.*	*ref.*
Miscellaneous industries	0.20	0.20	0.33	0.34	0.11	–0.55	–0.27	0.16	0.06	0.39
Crafts company?										
Yes	0.05	0.00	–0.15	0.05	–0.12	0.04	–0.28***	–0.11	0.05	–0.03
No	*ref.*	*ref.*	*ref.*	*ref.*	*ref.*	*ref.*	*ref.*	*ref.*	*ref.*	*ref.*
Intercept	–0.44**	–0.65***	–0.92***	–1.97***	–2.53***	–2.35***	–0.34*	–0.80***	–0.86***	–1.13***
n	934	934	934	934	934	934	934	934	934	934
Pseudo-R^2	0.084	0.095	0.087	0.134	0.170	0.166	0.079	0.039	0.070	0.037

Notes: *** / ** / * indicate statistical significance at the 1 percent / 5 percent / 10 percent levels respectively, based on heteroscedasticity-robust standard errors.

Source: IWH survey on firms in Thuringia, 2008.

There are signs that a large portion of these commuters are willing to pick up a job in Thuringia, given that the work conditions are acceptable. Secondly, female full-time employment could be increased. A prerequisite for using this resource calls for a reconciliation of work and family, which has to be supported by both the company and municipal authorities (e.g., full-time kindergarten and elementary school programs, flexible working hours, family-oriented personnel management programs). Thirdly, the large number of unemployed young adults and long-term unemployed people could be accessed as potential resources. Reactivation strategies, modularly organized requalification programs, might be helpful tools for a successful integration of these groups into the local labor markets.

Compared to West Germany, firms in Thuringia do not consider immigration of foreigners as a preferred strategy for overcoming the possible threat of skill shortage (Buscher et al. 2008). Our forecast indicates the greatest demand in the group of workers with a vocational education (rather than academics), and for this group the income hurdle associated with the current national immigration regulations appears much too high.

The second category of policies deals with education in a broader sense, including teaching at schools, universities, and vocational training. Even though Thuringia has reached a top position among German states in the PISA survey of the OECD, the state shares many of the deficiencies of the German school system: low permeability, the missing link between secondary school and the "world of work", and a considerable drop-out rate (7 percent of all pupils in Thuringia). Possible actions in this field include an upgrading of kindergarten education to lay the foundations for equal learning opportunities upon entering regular elementary schools. Such programs have shown to be effective in increasing student performance in later grades (Heckman 2000). Considering the high demand for engineering professions and the natural sciences, it would be reasonable to stir the curiosity of children (of both sexes) in these fields and thus to motivate them to follow a related career path.

The third category of measures is "information and consulting strategy". Small firms are often confronted with limited financial buffers, making it difficult for them to deal with uncertain future events. Limited financial resources may also lead to some restrictions in the context of offering wage premiums to attract qualified employees. Yet, there might be a chance of overcoming this disadvantage by offering different perks. Among others, one might think of flexible working-time arrangements, family-oriented employment conditions with childcare facilities, but also partly participation in the decision process of the firm, and medium-term perspectives of job protection. After all, there is a need to acknowledge that employees are a useful resource for the firm rather than just being part of the cost structure. In addition, some small firms are unable to offer apprenticeships because their work tasks do not cover all the training requirements for obtaining a vocational degree. Training networks across firms in partnership with educational institutions and chambers of commerce and industry provide a promising tool for overcoming such obstacles. Some arrangements of this kind have existed in the recent past as an instrument to address a shortage of apprenticeship positions supplied. While the market conditions for apprenticeships are turning into the opposite, support for such networks should be maintained into the future to help small firms meet their skilled-labor demand.

Another problem related to information deficits is the high drop-out rate of vocational training: 21 percent in 2007. This rate indicates that a large number of pupils have unrealistic expectations about their future job. However, this figure is also an indication of not yet fully used potentials in the field of vocational choice counseling. Here it seems necessary to install networks which inform pupils early about the requirements of the occupations they want to practice in the future. Such networks should involve vocational schools, firms, parents, and members of labor agencies. They should offer a wide range of possibilities for gaining practical experience to understand the requirements in various occupational fields and compare them with their personal preferences and talents.

As we have laid out, there exist a couple of strategies that could be initiated by local government and other key-actors within and outside the sphere of the firm to prepare the Thuringian economy for the impending repercussions of demographic change.

References

Beekman, T. / *Dekker,* R. J. / *de Grip,* A. / *Heijke,* J. A. (1991): "An explanation of the educational structure of occupations," Labour 5, 151–63.

Bellmann, L. (1997): "The IAB establishment panel with an exemplary analysis of employment expectations," IAB Labour Market Research Topics 20.

Blaug, M. (1967): "Approaches to educational planning," The Economic Journal 76, 262–87.

Bonin, H. / *Schneider,* M. / *Quinke,* H. / *Arens,* T. (2007). "Zukunft von Bildung und Arbeit. Perspektiven von Arbeitskräftebedarf und -angebot bis 2020." IZA Research Report 9.

Buscher, H. S. / *Reinowski,* E. / *Schmeißer,* C. / *Sunder,* M. / *Trocka,* D. (2008): Entwicklung des Fachkräftebedarfs in Thüringen – Fortschreibung Jahr 2008, Erfurt: Thüringer Ministerium für Wirtschaft, Technologie und Arbeit (TMWTA).

Fuchs, J. / *Söhnlein,* D. (2005): "Vorausschätzung der Erwerbsbevölkerung bis 2050," IAB-Forschungsbericht 16 / 2005, Institute for Employment Research, Germany.

Heckman, J. J. (2000): "Policies to foster human capital," Research in Economics 54 (1), 3–56.

Kubis, A. N. / *Schneider,* L. (2007): "'Sag mir, wo die Mädchen sind ...' Regionale Analyse des Wanderungsverhaltens junger Frauen," Wirtschaft im Wandel 13 (8), 298–307.

Meyer, B. / *Lutz,* C. / *Schnur,* P. / *Zika,* G. (2007): "National economic policy simulations with global interdependencies. A sensitivity analysis for Germany," Economic Systems Research 19 (1), 37–55.

Reinberg, A. / *Hummel,* M. (2002): "Zur langfristigen Entwicklung des qualifikationsspezifischen Arbeitskräfteangebots und -bedarfs in Deutschland. Empirische Befunde und aktuelle Projektionsergebnisse," Mitteilungen aus der Arbeitsmarkt- und Berufsforschung 35 (4), 580–600.

Schömann, K. / *Gülker,* S. / *Hilbert,* C. (2000): Qualifikationsbedarf in den Ländern der OECD – Ermittlung, Analysen und Implementation, Bielefeld: Bertelsmann-Verlag.

Statistisches Bundesamt (2006): "Bevölkerung Deutschlands bis 2050. 11. koordinierte Bevölkerungsvorausberechnung." Wiesbaden: Statistisches Bundesamt.

Veneri, C. M. (1999): "Can occupational labor shortages be identified using available data," Monthly Labor Review 122, 15–21.

Will There Be a Shortage of Skilled Labor? An East German Perspective to 2015

Comment

By Hilmar Schneider*

General Remarks

The paper by Buscher et al. addresses a hot debate in Germany about the threat of a potential skilled-labor gap caused by demographic factors. It follows a simple pragmatic approach based on the so-called manpower requirement method. This is useful, in order to get an impression of future changes of labor supply and labor demand by extrapolating demographic shifts and employment trends under the assumption that economic actors do not adjust their behavior. The method is able to indicate potential need for adjustment and policy interventions.

The analysis is carried out for the East German State of Thuringia. This is motivated by the fact that demographic shifts are especially pronounced in East Germany as a whole. A massive birth decline at the beginning of the 1990s is about to unfold noticeable consequences on the labor market. If such demographic shifts are likely to cause an increased mismatch between skill specific demand and supply, this should particularly become a problem in East Germany.

However, it might as well be the case, that demographic shifts could alleviate the labor market situation. Given the extraordinary high level of unemployment in East Germany, it is not a priori clear, whether mismatch is a problem at all in this region. This points to a general weakness of the paper: Instead of trying to question and quantify the empirical substance of a potential skill gap in an economical sense, it simply takes the assumption of a skill gap as given. The only evidence relies on a firm survey asking for perceived recruitment difficulties, which is definitely not sufficient. Even if firms are claiming recruitment difficulties, the price dimension of the problem is fully neglected. The crucial questions are, would these firms be able to get the required workers if they were willing to pay higher wages as they do, and if so, why don't they pay such wages? It might well turn out that the truth behind a problem labeled as skill gap is a lack of competitiveness of firms.

---

* Institute for the Study of Labor (IZA), Bonn, Germany. German Institute for Economic Research (DIW), Berlin, Germany. Corresponding address: PD Dr. Hilmar Schneider, IZA, Postfach 2340, D-53072 Bonn. E-mail address: schneider@iza.org.

Moreover, it is not fully clear how the results presented in the first section of the paper are related to the results presented in the second part of the paper. The first section starts out with a mechanical assessment of the demographical impact on the supply of skills and confronts this with a trend projection of skill demand. Surprisingly, the strongest divergence between supply and demand is to be expected for low skilled workers. The supply of low skilled workers is declining twice as strong as the supply of academics (see Figure 3 of the paper). However, the overall decline of the projected gap between supply and demand is by far less than the number of unemployed. One could therefore conclude here that demography is unlikely to produce serious problems in the East German labor market.

Instead, however, this section is followed by an empirical analysis of recruitment difficulties faced by firms. With this step, the authors want to provide evidence that recruitment difficulties are an issue for firms already today. In the same survey, firms where asked about recruitment difficulties expected in the near future and how they are preparing for them. This doesn't make sense, if the results of the first section hold. Nevertheless, there seem to be firms that arc expecting increasing recruitment difficulties in the future. However, this is not linked to the overall projection of the potential skill gap in the preceding section.

Remarks in Particular

Projection of labor supply

The projection of labor supply is based on variant 1 of the 11th coordinated population projection of the Federal Statistical Office. Among else, this projection assumes a net immigration of 100,000 people per year. The actual figure since 2004 has only reached about 60,000 people per year and it can be doubted, whether the projected number will be reached in the years to come. As a result, the decline of labor supply might be slightly underestimated.

The way, how the population projection is weighted by age-specific qualification structure sounds contradictory with regard to the treatment of individuals still in the educational system. On the one hand, the paper states that for individuals aged between 15 and 29 as a remedy the qualification structure of individuals between 30 and 39 is applied. On the other hand, the paper states that for individuals in a certain type of education, it is assumed that they will achieve the corresponding level of qualification. However, both strategies cannot be applied together without a dominance rule, which remains unexplained. Moreover, it remains unclear, from what simulation period on individuals attending an educational institution at the beginning of the simulation period will be regarded as having completed their education.

The projection of skill specific labor supply is not only based on a given distribution of age-specific skill levels but also on a given distribution of skill and age-specific participation rates. However, while the skill structure may be viewed as fixed, participation rates are more subject to intertemporal decision making and thus open an element of flexibility. It would have been interesting to get an impression on the flexibility buffer that could be mobilized by changes in participation rates. This is especially true for a reduction of early retirement age. Beyond this, it would have been interesting to learn something about the flexibility buffer that arises from an extraordinary high proportion of out-commuters to states in the Western neighborhood.[1] Both would have likely underpinned that the threat of a skilled-labor gap is far from serious or at least manageable.

Projection of labor demand

The projection of labor demand consists of a projection of replacement demand and a projection of overall labor demand. However, the quantification of replacement demand is of minor importance for the general question addressed in the paper. It simply tells how many vacancies might arise from the fact that a certain amount of workers will retire during the projection period. This has nothing to say with regard to a potential skill gap.

The trend projection of overall labor demand is based on a relatively short observation period (2003–2007). The reason for this has to be seen in the huge but unique structural changes in Eastern Germany, which took place during the nineties and cannot be extrapolated into the future. Unfortunately, details of the estimation procedure are hidden in a black box. The outcome results in a predicted overall decline of labor demand of approximately 10,000 employees until 2015.

The main problem of the projection of labor demand consists of a conceptual inconsistency with the projection of labor supply. While the projection of labor supply is based on the ILO labor force concept, the projection of labor demand is based on employment subject to social security contributions (ESSSC). ESSSC is covering roughly 70% of overall employment. The problem arises from a continuous shift in the composition of labor demand (Figure 1). While ESSSC is steadily losing ground, alternative forms of employment like self-employment and so-called minijobs are advancing. The overall labor demand has rather been increasing during the reference period, which is indicated by a slight expansion of hours worked by 0.35%, in Thuringia between 2003 and 2007.[2] However, ESSSC has been declining by 2.5%.[3]

---

1 According to official figures provided by the Federal Labor Agency almost 12% of workers subject to social security contributions living in Thuringia are working in West Germany. This is the highest proportion of out-commuting to West Germany among all German Federal states. Own computation based on the following source: http://www.pub.arbeitsamt.de/hst/services/statistik/200812/iiia6/pendler/blxbld.xls.

2 Own computation based on figures provided by the Arbeitskreis "Erwerbstätigenrechnung des Bundes und der Länder" at (http://www.statistik-hessen.de/erwerbstaetigenrechnung/arbeitsstunden.htm).

3 Own computation based on official figures provided by the Federal Labor Agency (Sources: http://www.pub.arbeitsamt.de/hst/services/statistik/200312/iiia6/pendler/blxbld.xls and http://www.pub.arbeitsamt.de/hst/services/statistik/200712/iiia6/pendler/blxbld.xls).

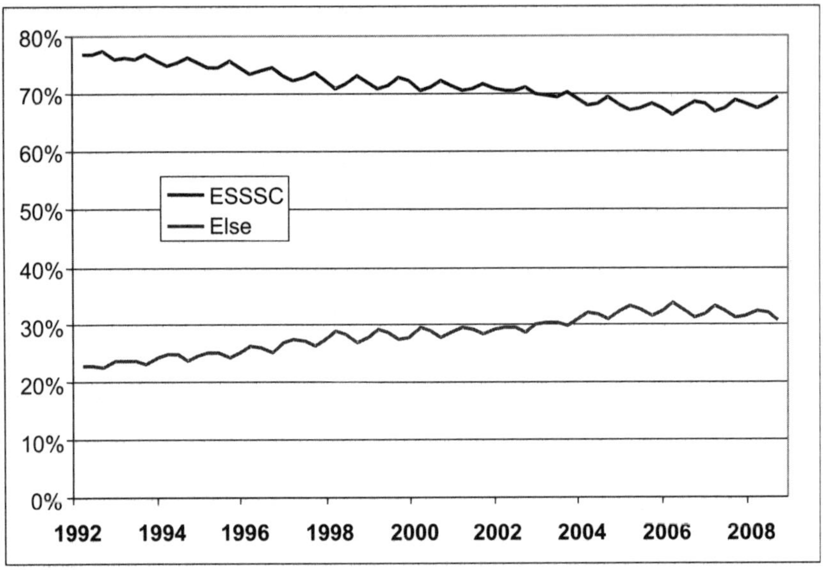

Remark: ESSSC stands for "employment subject to social security contributions".
Source: Federal Statistical Office, Federal Labor Agency.

Figure 1: Composition of Employment over Time

Using the same employment concept for the projection of labor demand as being used for the projection of labor supply would probably have led to a somewhat different conclusion with regard to the potential skill gap. There is no obvious reason for the usage of two different employment concepts for projection. For example, the projection of labor demand could as well have been based on Microcensus data, which would have led to consistent projections.

The perspective of firms

As already mentioned, the section covering firm's attitudes towards shortages of skilled labor is somewhat unrelated to the projection part of the paper. An implicit assumption being made seems to be that an already existing shortage of skilled labor might increase if labor supply declines relative to labor demand. However, this must not necessarily be the case. The missing link is an explanation to the question why vacancies cannot be filled despite a high excess labor supply. It could be low quality of labor supply, but this might change in the future independently from quantitative changes of supply and demand. It could also be a problem of wages, which might change independently from demographic processes as well. The economic meaning of a skill shortage points to a strand of mismatch literature that became prominent during the 1980s. For Germany, this has primarily been captured in papers by Franz and König (e.g. Franz/König 1986, Franz

1987). The mismatch approach would have been worth considering for the present paper as well.

Conclusion

Diagnosing a skill mismatch is obviously not as easy as it may look at first sight. The paper by Buscher et al. provides contradictory results based on two conceptually different approaches. On the one hand, the (more mechanical) manpower requirement approach does not indicate need for action according to a projected reduction of the gap between supply and demand far below the existing supply buffer. On the other hand, firms are claiming a lack of skilled workers already today, despite a large excess supply of skilled workers. If this were true, even a slight reduction of excess labor supply might aggravate recruitment problems in the future. However, a crucial question remains unanswered: What is a skill shortage?

References

Franz, W. (1987): "Strukturelle und friktionelle Arbeitslosigkeit in der Bundesrepublik Deutschland. Eine theoretische und empirische Analyse der Beveridge-Kurve," in: G. Bombach, B. Gahlen u. A. E. Ott, (Hrsg.): Arbeitsmärkte und Beschäftigung – Fakten, Analysen, Perspektiven, Mohr und Siebeck, Tübingen, 301 – 323.

Franz, W. / *König,* H. (1986): "The Nature and Causes of Unemployment in the Federal Republic of Germany since the 1970s: An Empirical Investigation," Economica (Supplement) 53, 219 – 244.

Returns to Human Capital in Germany Post-Unification

By Katie Lupo* and Silke Anger**

Abstract

Following German unification in 1990, a number of initial studies were conducted on the development of the returns to education in the eastern states of the former GDR. These studies reveal a general consensus of initial falls in the returns to education for the eastern states (Krueger and Pischke 1992; Bird, Schwarze and Wagner 1994) before beginning to raise towards western levels. This study examines the development of returns to human capital for the eastern states following unification. Data from the German Socio Economic Panel Study is used to compare the eastern and western returns to human capital during the transition years of 1989 until 1991, followed by a longitudinal analysis until 2007 investigating returns to schooling and work experience, differentiating between experience in the GDR and work experience obtained outside of the GDR. In addition to returns to years of schooling, returns to specific degrees are examined. Results show an initial decline in the returns to human capital for easterners, followed by a relatively steady incline. Returns to education for eastern women reached western levels soon after unification, but returns for eastern men took until 2005 to achieve the levels of western men.

JEL Classification: I21, J24, R23

Keywords: returns to human capital, education, experience, wage inequality

1. Introduction

It is widely accepted that additional years of schooling have positive impacts on an individual's wage in the labor market. This has been explained in the literature as the return to human capital, dating back to Becker (1964) and Mincer (1974). German unification provided a natural experiment of how human capital obtained under communism would be rewarded in a free-market economy. Following unification, the eastern German wage structure was completely transformed. Under socialism,

* *Corresponding author.* Wisconsin Center for Education Research, School of Education, University of Wisconsin-Madison, Madison, Wisconsin, USA. E-mail address: lupo@wisc.edu.

** DIW Berlin, Mohrenstraße 58, 10117 Berlin.
The authors thank seminar participants in the SOEP Brownbag seminar for their helpful comments. Katie Lupo would like to thank the German Institute for Economic Research for their help and input and the Fulbright Commission for the financial resources to complete this study. All remaining errors are our own.

the wage structure was extremely compressed, and wages were relatively independent of educational background. Therefore with the onset of a free market economy, one could expect changes in the wages based on human capital. At the same time, some of the human capital obtained in socialism became obsolete. This raises the question of how the returns to human capital have evolved since unification. There is some existing literature regarding the initial changes in the returns to human capital in the early transition years, but there is a lack of analysis pertaining to the changes over time.

Using data from the German Socio-Economics Panel Study (SOEP), this paper uses Mincer type earnings equations controlling for selection into the labor force for eastern and western males and females from 1989 through 2007. These models are used to show the returns to education, experience and specific school-leaving degrees separately for eastern and western Germans. The initial transition years of 1989 through 1991 are examined in a similar fashion to Bird, Schwarze and Wagner (1994) and Krueger and Pischke (1992). Next, the returns to education and experience are interacted with year dummy variables to look at changes over time. As Germany has a unique tiered schooling system, returns to specific school leaving degrees are also examined.

The paper is organized as follows. The first section provides an overview of the existing literature in regards to the return to education in Germany post-unification. The second section explains the data and methods used for the models. The results are then presented in the third section, followed by a concluding discussion.

2. Literature Review

Initial studies on the returns to human capital in the eastern German states in the years just before unification have varied results. Schwarze (1991a) and Schwarze (1991b) accessed income data from the GDR from the Survey of Blue- and White Collar Households, from which returns to education of approximately 5.6 percent were calculated using standard OLS models. Bird, Schwarze and Wagner (1994) evaluate the transition towards free markets in East Germany and find returns of 4.4 percent per year of education in 1989, actually falling to 4.1 percent in 1991. On the contrary, Krueger and Pischke (1992) find returns in the eastern states of 7 to 8 percent in the years directly following unification. Looking at the differences in returns for specific school degree, they find the returns in the West were higher for specific school leaving degrees. They argue that this may be due the fact that schooling took more years in West Germany, which subsequently would lower the returns to each additional year of schooling.

There are a limited number of studies, which examine the evolution of the returns to wages in eastern and western Germany post-unification. Ammermüller and Weber (2005) examine the returns to education for men and women separately in the eastern and western states between 1992 and 2002. Results for 1992 provide differences in educational returns between eastern (6.08 percent) and western states (8.39 percent) which decrease to only 0.46 percentage points in 2002. The returns for eastern women (8.78 percent) were even 0.90 percentage points higher than those of western women (7.68 percent) by 2002. Though the actual rates differ, Gang and Yun (2003) also find a trend of increasing returns to human capital for easterners with the rate of return to schooling rising from 3.9 percent in 1990 to 5.2 percent in 2000.

Work has been done in other transitional economies and rising returns to education have been found after the collapse of communism. Chase (1997) uses cross-sectional data for 1984 and 1993 in the Czech Republic and Slovakia to find rising returns for both men and women in both countries. Münich, Svejnar and Terrell (2005) find similar results for the Czech Republic rising from 2.7 percent in 1990 to 5.8 percent in 1996. Orazem and Vodopivec (1995) look at the returns for different school leaving degrees in Slovenia and find large increases between 1987 and 1999.

Most existing studies which focus on the returns to education in Germany after re-unification use cross-sectional data. While this provides valuable information regarding the economic impact of educational attainment, it does not allow one to examine the changes in the returns to human capital over time. Therefore, this study adds to the literature by following the same large sample of East and West Germans for nineteen years (1989–2007) and observing how returns to human capital for these same individuals changed before, during and after reunification. Furthermore, it explicitly distinguishes between pre- and post-unification human capital and compares returns to work experience acquired before unification with returns after unification.

3. Data

The data used in this study were taken from the German-Socio Economic Panel (SOEP) data for the years 1989–2007. The SOEP is a representative sample of German households and individuals, and data have been collected for former West Germany since 1984, with the addition of an eastern sample in 1990. Since 1990, additional groups have been added, such as a sample of immigrants, a high income sample, and refreshment samples (Wagner, Frick and Schupp 2007). This study concerns itself with the German education system, and samples of foreigners living in Germany are excluded from the sample.[1] One of the most prominent features of the data set is its large and stable size, which enables longitudinal analysis to account for compositional changes. A possible problem with the data, however, is that using a longitudinal sample creates the possibility for attrition bias, i.e., individuals dropping out of the survey.[2]

1 Samples used include wave A, C, E, F, and H from the SOEP dataset.

2 Studies concerning the attrition bias of the SOEP point to problems with unsuccessful follow-up interviews (e. g. household moves, separation of households, etc.). Divorce, residing in East Berlin, and job loss have all been linked to a reduced rate of responding to follow-up waves of the survey. For more information, see Haisken-DeNew and Frick, 2005.

Before discussing the variables used, it should be noted that this study considers only individuals who should be finished with their studies in order to reduce possible bias. Therefore it is limited to citizens between the ages of 25 and 60. Furthermore, employment for the purposes of this study is restricted to full-time employment, which is defined as those claiming to be full-time employed *and* currently working more than 25 hours a week. Individuals claiming to be self-employed and those employed fulltime with missing information are not included in the study. A description of the variables for those employed can be found in Table 1.

Table 1

Descriptive Statistics

Variable	West		East		Migrants*	
	Mean	Std. Dev.	Mean	Std. Dev.	Mean	Std. Dev.
Monthly gross income (euros)	3006.11	1537.57	1798.33	973.27	2604.77	1156.22
Female	0.28	0.45	0.41	0.49	0.39	0.49
Years of education	12.31	2.67	12.73	2.41	13.00	2.58
University degree	0.21	0.40	0.32	0.47	0.28	0.45
Technical school degree	0.24	0.43	0.15	0.36	0.17	0.38
High school degree	0.06	0.23	0.03	0.16	0.07	0.25
Apprenticeship	0.41	0.49	0.47	0.50	0.44	0.50
Experience	18.27	10.18	19.13	9.66	15.50	10.06
Experience before 1990	10.50	9.51	12.64	9.47	7.30	8.37
Experience from 1990	7.78	4.78	6.53	4.76	8.20	4.21
Tenure	12.36	10.07	10.10	9.46	5.71	5.70
Weekly working hours	42.94	6.64	44.55	7.00	43.97	7.55
Public sector	0.29	0.46	0.33	0.47	0.20	0.40
Large firm (> 2000 employees)	0.26	0.44	0.23	0.42	0.21	0.41
Number of kids in household	0.66	0.96	0.74	0.89	0.47	0.75
Married	0.64	0.48	0.73	0.44	0.53	0.50
Age	41.13	9.54	41.60	9.25	38.01	9.67
Observations	46,825		25,631		1,910	

Source: SOEP 1990 – 2007.

* Migrants are defined as those who grew up in the eastern states and moved to the western states after unification.

The dependent variable measured is the gross monthly wages and bonus payments, including vacation money, profit sharing, holiday bonuses, and thirteenth and fourteenth month's pay. Table 1 shows the average gross monthly income for western Germans to be higher than that of eastern Germans using pooled data from 1991 until 2007 (3,006 euros versus 1,798, respectively). As control variables we use weekly hours worked, formal education, work experience, tenure, employment in the public sector, firm size, and region. All the regressions are run separately for males and females. Table 1 shows that in comparison to the western German labor force, a higher percentage of the eastern German full-time workers is female (28 percent and 41 percent, respectively). While the average tenure is lower in the eastern states (10.1 years) than in the western states (12.36 years), work experience is higher. The average total work experience in the eastern states is 19.1 years in comparison to only 18.3 years in the western states. This can be explained by the guaranteed employment of East Germans under the control of the German Democratic Republic (GDR). Furthermore, eastern Germans have a lower average number of years of work experience after the fall of the GDR, which can be explained as a result of career interruptions and unemployment spells due to the restructuring process during transition. It is also interesting to note that eastern Germans have on average slightly more years of schooling (12.7) than western Germans (12.3). The percentage of eastern Germans with a university degree is 32 percent, while only 21 percent of western Germans hold a university degree. Only 1 percent of eastern and western Germans have no further education after high school. Hence, high school graduates with and without an additional vocational degree are grouped together. In addition to the independent observable variables, the number of children present in the household, marital status, and age are included as selection variables for selection into fulltime employment.

4. Empirical Strategy

To estimate the returns to human capital in the eastern and western states, following the work of Bird, Schwarze and Wagner (1994) we employ ordinary least squares earnings equations on cross-sectional data from 1989 until 1991 based on Mincer (1974). This allows for comparison of the returns to human capital in the German Democratic Republic (GDR) with those of the Federal Republic of Germany (FRG) before re-unification and an initial glimpse of the situation after re-unification. Using ordinary least squares,

$$\text{(1)} \qquad \ln y = \beta_0 + \beta_1 * Experience + \beta_2 Experience^2 + \beta_3 Schooling + \varepsilon$$

where schooling refers to years of *schooling* and *experience* to years of fulltime work experience. Moving on, we examine the changes in the returns to experience and education in the years after re-unification are also examined. A variation on the Mincer wage equation is used

(2)

$$\ln y = \beta_0 + \beta_1 * Controls + \delta_{ij} Schooling + \lambda_{ij} Experience + \gamma_{ij} Experience^2 + \varphi_i Year + \varepsilon$$

where *year* is interacted with education or experience and *controls* is a vector of control variables for firm size, public sector employment, and hours worked. *Experience* is then broken down into experience pre- and post-unification in order to test whether experience obtained under the East German communist regime is rewarded the same as experience under capitalism. In the last model, instead of implementing the years of schooling, we also look at the returns to specific school leaving degrees. The main problem with these estimates arises from bias due to unobservable factors influencing educational attainment and selection into the workforce. In order to control for such factors and eliminate any correlations amongst the error terms, we employ a Heckman (1979) selection model using age, marital status and the number of children present in the household for selection into the workforce. Estimates are performed separately for eastern and western women and men.

5. Results

5.1 Initial Transition Years

A first glimpse at the returns to education and experience in the early transition years uncover differences between eastern and western males and females. OLS estimates with and without controlling for selection can be found in Tables 2 and 3. Results for and without controlling for selectivity are presented for the early transition years, and given the significance of the selectivity term in most specifications, subsequent results are only shown with selection controls.

Returns to education and experience fell for all easterners upon the onset of the free-market economy. Returns for eastern men began and remained well below those of western men throughout the initial years of transition. In 1989, men saw returns of only 6 percent for each additional year of schooling. By 1991, returns fell for easterners a full 1.1 percentage points while they fell only 0.9 percentage points for western men. Similar results were found using OLS estimates by Bird, Schwarze and Wagner (1994) and Krueger and Pischke (1992). Controlling for selection has little effect on the coefficients for men, as can be seen by results presented on the right hand side of Table 2. The drop in returns to education in the eastern states following unification can be explained as the initial shock brought on by the free-market economy. Meanwhile the fall in the western states may be due to the shock brought about by the sudden massive increase in the size of the German labor force. Returns to experience were also lower for eastern men and fell in the first year of re-unification (from 1.3 percent to 1.0 percent) before increasing to 1.5 percent in 1991. Western returns to experience began well above eastern levels (3.9 percent in 1989) and followed a trend similar to easterners falling to 3.5 percent in 1991 and rising to 3.7 percent by 1991. While the selection term is statistically significant in the estimates for western males, selection does not seem to play a big role for eastern full-time working men.

Similar results are seen in the returns to human capital for eastern and western women. Results are presented in Table 3, where it can be seen that simple OLS estimates without selection controls are positively biased for western. Returns to education for western women between 1989 and 1991 ranged from 8.7 to 9.7 percent without controlling for selection, whereas controls reduce the returns to 7.8 to 8.9 percent. This could be explained by the differences in eastern and western work ethics. Women in the western states are more likely to leave the workforce in order to raise a family, therefore negatively selecting out of the labor force.

Table 2: **Returns to Human Capital in the Initial Transition Years: Males**

	Ordinary Least Squares						Heckman Selection Model					
	West			East			West			East		
	1989	1990	1991	1989	1990	1991	1989	1990	1991	1989	1990	1991
Years of Education	0.080**	0.076**	0.071**	0.060**	0.054**	0.049**	0.080**	0.077**	0.071**	0.059**	0.053**	0.049**
	(0.003)	(0.003)	(0.003)	(0.003)	(0.003)	(0.005)	(0.003)	(0.003)	(0.003)	(0.003)	(0.003)	(0.004)
Full-time Experience	0.041**	0.0372**	0.037**	0.014**	0.011**	0.015**	0.039**	0.035**	0.037**	0.013**	0.010**	0.015**
	(0.003)	(0.003)	(0.003)	(0.003)	(0.003)	(0.004)	(0.003)	(0.003)	(0.003)	(0.003)	(0.003)	(0.004)
Full-time Experience squ.	–0.001**	–0.000**	–0.000**	–0.022**	–0.000**	–0.000**	–0.001**	–0.001**	–0.001**	–0.019**	–0.000**	–0.000**
	(0.000)	(0.000)	(0.000)	(0.006)	(0.000)	(0.000)	(0.000)	(0.000)	(0.000)	(0.006)	(0.000)	(0.000)
Constant	6.283**	6.396**	6.486**	6.220**	5.710**	6.062**	6.372**	6.493**	6.589**	6.330**	5.777**	6.093**
	(0.047)	(0.047)	(0.047)	(0.044)	(0.046)	(0.070)	(0.050)	(0.052)	(0.054)	(0.045)	(0.050)	(0.080)
Adjusted R-squared	0.34	0.32	0.30	0.30	0.23	0.12						
Lambda							–0.0833	–0.0977	–0.0938	–0.0485	–0.0429	–0.0415
							(0.0132)	(0.0192)	(0.0159)	(0.0137)	(0.0161)	(0.0243)
Wald test of indep. equations							6.848	7.488	6.691	0.347	0.522	0.275
Observations	1,688	1,626	1,617	1,103	1,129	932	1,688	1,626	1,617	1,103	1,129	932

Notes: Robust standard errors in parentheses, ** $p < 0.05$.

Source: SOEP 1989 – 1991.

After controlling for selection, results show that the returns to education for eastern and western women were nearly the same at the end of the German Democratic Republic (GDR) with 9.0 and 8.9 percent, respectively. In the first year after the fall of communism, returns for eastern women dropped slightly to 8.4 percent per year of education, and they fell to 7.8 percent for western women. In the eastern states, the downward trend continued to 6.5 percent in 1991, while in the western states they rose to 8.2 percent. Returns to experience also remained stable in the eastern states between 1989 and 1990 at 2.7 percent, before falling to 1.6 percent in 1991. Returns to experience in the western states remained between 4 and 5 percent. The changes in returns to human capital in the Eastern states can be explained as the transition of the worth of human capital obtained under the GRD to the free-market system.

5.2 Returns to Experience

The returns to experience and tenure within a firm can be seen in Tables 4 and 5. Controlling for selection into the workforce based on age, the number of children present in the household and marital status, results are based on a simple Mincer (1974) style OLS model. Table 4 presents results for eastern and western males and females in the form of returns to tenure within a firm and returns to work experience interacted with year dummy variables.[3] This enables the analysis of the changes in the returns to work experience after unification in the eastern and western states. Results in Table 4 show that the returns to each additional year of tenure within a firm are comparable for workers in the western and the eastern states during the years 1990 to 2007. Male workers and West German women are shown to earn approximately 1.4 percent more for each additional year of tenure, while eastern females earn a slightly higher return of an additional 1.9 percent. This could be a possible effect of the wage structure in the former GDR and the fixed salary increases with additional years of work, which seems more relevant for women. Those remaining in the same firm see these rewards, while those who have changed jobs do not realize these compensations.

Table 4 also presents the returns to work experience in each year from 1990 until 2007. Returns to work experience began and remained clearly higher for western males and females. In 1990, the rate of return started at 2.3 percent for males and at 2.6 percent for females in West Germany, and rose slightly over time to reach approximately 3.5 percent in 2007. In the same time period, the rate of return grew for eastern men though never reaching western levels. The return per year of work experience began at 0.5 percent (although not statistically significant) for eastern men and 1.1 percent for eastern women in 1990. This rate had an initial fall for males to a low of about zero percent in 1992 to 1995 before increasing to 1.0 percent by 2000.

---

[3] Total work experience has been calculated by summing up full-time and part-time experience of a worker. The years of part-time work experience have been divided by two.

Table 3: **Returns to Human Capital in the Initial Transition Years: Females**

	OLS						Selection					
	West			East			West			East		
	1989	1990	1991	1989	1990	1991	1989	1990	1991	1989	1990	1991
Years of Education	0.097**	0.087**	0.087**	.0902**	0.084**	0.067**	0.089**	0.078**	0.082**	0.090**	0.084**	0.065**
	(0.006)	(0.006)	(0.006)	(0.004)	(0.005)	(0.005)	(0.005)	(0.005)	(0.005)	(0.004)	(0.004)	(0.005)
Full-time Experience	0.048**	0.045**	0.050**	.026577**	0.027**	0.017**	0.046**	0.041**	0.049**	0.027**	0.027**	0.016**
	(0.005)	(0.005)	(0.005)	(0.003)	(0.003)	(0.004)	(0.004)	(0.004)	(0.004)	(0.003)	(0.003)	(0.004)
Full-time Experience squ.	–0.001**	–0.001**	–0.001**	–0,04463**	–0.001**	–0.001**	–0.001**	–0.001**	–0.001**	–0.045**	–0.001**	–0.001**
	(0.000)	(0.000)	(0.000)	(0.008)	(0.000)	(0.000)	(0.000)	(0.000)	(0.000)	(0.008)	(0.000)	(0.000)
Constant	5.692**	5.843**	5.878**	5,456991**	4.916**	5.502**	6.211**	6.579**	6.365**	5.422**	4.890**	5.755**
	(0.076)	(0.081)	(0.076)	(0.0610)	(0.064)	(0.072)	(0.094)	(0.084)	(0.083)	(0.072)	(0.073)	(0.078)
Adjusted R-squared	0.37	0.30	0.32	0,3321	0.28	0.21						
Lambda							–0.0741	–0.0867	–0.0721	–0.128	–0.159	0.0185
							(0.0245)	(0.0326)	(0.0268)	(0.0827)	(0.0827)	(0.0832)
Wald test of indep. equations							8.699	9.949	6.319	2.413	2.783	0.0317
Observations	764	793	831	998	1,053	818	2,511	2,467	2,483	1,584	1,639	1,570

Notes: Robust standard errors in parentheses, ** $p < 0.05$.

Source: SOEP 1989 – 1991.

Table 4

Returns to Experience by Region and Gender

	Males		Females	
	West	East	West	East
Years of Education	0.080*** (0.001)	0.066*** (0.001)	0.071*** (0.001)	0.072*** (0.001)
Tenure	0.015*** (0.001)	0.014*** (0.001)	0.013*** (0.001)	0.019*** (0.001)
Tenure squ.	–0.000*** (0.000)	–0.000*** (0.000)	–0.000*** (0.000)	–0.000*** (0.000)
Experience	0.023*** (0.003)	0.005 (0.003)	0.026*** (0.005)	0.011*** (0.004)
Experience*1991	0.003 (0.004)	–0.001 (0.005)	0.001 (0.007)	–0.010* (0.006)
Experience*1992	–0.000 (0.004)	–0.004 (0.007)	0.008 (0.007)	0.011 (0.008)
Experience*1993	–0.000 (0.004)	–0.007 (0.005)	–0.010 (0.007)	0.001 (0.007)
Experience*1994	–0.002 (0.004)	–0.005 (0.006)	0.002 (0.007)	0.001 (0.007)
Experience*1995	0.005 (0.004)	–0.004 (0.006)	0.009 (0.007)	0.002 (0.007)
Experience*1996	0.005 (0.004)	0.002 (0.006)	0.006 (0.007)	–0.005 (0.007)
Experience*1997	0.006 (0.004)	0.002 (0.005)	0.013* (0.008)	–0.004 (0.007)
Experience*1998	0.004 (0.004)	0.004 (0.006)	0.005 (0.007)	–0.004 (0.007)
Experience*1999	0.003 (0.004)	0.002 (0.006)	0.007 (0.007)	0.002 (0.006)
Experience*2000	0.006 (0.004)	0.005 (0.005)	–0.000 (0.006)	0.012** (0.006)
Experience*2001	0.002 (0.004)	0.005 (0.005)	–0.001 (0.006)	0.007 (0.007)
Experience*2002	0.005 (0.004)	0.009 (0.006)	0.007 (0.007)	0.011 (0.007)
Experience*2003	0.009** (0.004)	0.013** (0.006)	0.001 (0.007)	0.007 (0.007)
Experience*2004	0.011** (0.004)	0.008 (0.006)	0.004 (0.006)	0.013** (0.006)
Experience*2005	0.016*** (0.004)	0.018** (0.007)	0.004 (0.007)	0.015** (0.007)
Experience*2006	0.017*** (0.005)	0.018*** (0.006)	0.007 (0.007)	0.017** (0.007)
Experience*2007	0.013*** (0.004)	0.026*** (0.006)	0.011* (0.006)	0.016** (0.007)

Experience squ.	–0.001***	–0.001	–0.001***	–0.001***
	(0.000)	(0.000)	(0.000)	(0.000)
Constant	5.960***	5.116***	5.942***	4.682***
	(0.029)	(0.039)	(0.049)	(0.046)
Lambda	–0.158	–0.104	–0.0659	0.0316
	(0.009)	(0.019)	(0.009)	(0.016)
Wald test of indep. equations	296.8	44.73	80.30	1.914
Censored Obs.	11,124	6,350	36,628	12,970
Observations	44,681	21,356	49,896	23,595

Notes: Robust standard errors in parentheses, *** $p < 0.01$, ** $p < 0.05$, * $p < 0.1$. Dependent variable: log of gross monthly earnings, Additional controls: public sector, firm size, year dummies.

Source: SOEP 1990 – 2007.

The returns for work experience for eastern women remained between 1.0 and 2.0 percent in the early 1990s, and increased after a low at the end of the 1990s to around 2.5 percent after 2000. Much of the expertise acquired in the socialist German Democratic Republic was not of as high of a value in the capitalist system of western Germany. Therefore, it would be expected that it does not receive as favorable of returns. With the unification of the two markets, it could be expected that new skills would be acquired and the returns would increase for easterners over time. However, for workers in both East and West Germany, skills acquired at the workplace have become more valuable over time, as the growing rates of return to work experience show in both parts of Germany.

Next, Table 5 shows results for the returns to work experience differentiating between experience obtained before and after unification. Results are based on pooled data, controlling for the year, hours worked, formal education, tenure, firm size, and public sector employment. Results show that experience earned after unification is more valuable for both easterners and westerners. This finding is independent from the German unification, but a simple time effect, since newly obtained skills learned on-the-job yield higher returns than human capital which was accumulated at the work place many years ago and has already been depreciated. However, comparing West German and East German workers allows for conclusions with respect to the value of human capital acquired under the socialist market regime. For western men, returns to each year of employment before unification was 0.8 percent, while it is actually found to be a –0.7 percent for eastern males. Therefore, as a result of the unification, East German full-time workers were actually punished for every year of employment they had experienced under the socialist system. Experience obtained after unification is calculated to be 6.5 percent for western males and 4.6 percent for eastern males. Similar results are found for females, where experience before 1990 saw returns of 0.9 percent for westerners and no statistically significant returns for easterners. Post-unification returns were found to be 6.7 percent for western woman and 5.2 percent for easterners. These results clearly indicate that the experience obtained under socialism does not carry the same value of human capital obtained in the social-market system.

Table 5

Returns to GDR and Post-GDR Experience

	Males		Females	
	West	East	West	East
Years of Education	0.081***	0.067***	0.072***	0.071***
	(0.001)	(0.001)	(0.001)	(0.001)
Tenure	0.015***	0.012***	0.013***	0.015***
	(0.001)	(0.001)	(0.001)	(0.001)
Tenure squ.	–0.001***	–0.001***	–0.001***	–0.001***
	(0.000)	(0.000)	(0.000)	(0.000)
Experience before 1990	0.008***	–0.007***	0.009***	0.001
	(0.001)	(0.001)	(0.001)	(0.001)
Experience before 1990 squ.	–0.001***	0.001***	–0.001***	–0.001
	(0.000)	(0.000)	(0.000)	(0.000)
Experience from 1990	0.065***	0.046***	0.067***	0.052***
	(0.003)	(0.005)	(0.004)	(0.005)
Experience from 1990 squ.	–0.002***	–0.001***	–0.002***	–0.001***
	(0.000)	(0.000)	(0.000)	(0.000)
Constant	6.090***	5.234***	6.065***	4.806***
	(0.018)	(0.027)	(0.036)	(0.037)
Lambda	–0.153	–0.0787	–0.0362	0.0488
	(0.009)	(0.019)	(0.007)	(0.014)
Wald test of indep. equations	289.5	24.86	25.72	5.403
Censored Obs.	11,124	6,350	36,628	12,970
Observations	44,681	21,356	49,896	23,595

Notes: Robust standard errors in parentheses, *** $p < 0.01$, ** $p < 0.05$, * $p < 0.1$. Dependent variable: log of gross monthly earnings, Additional controls: public sector, firm size, year dummies.

Source: SOEP 1990 – 2007.

5.3 Returns to Education

The returns to education over time are presented separately for men and women in Table 6. Results are based on OLS controlling for selection into the labor force as well as for year, public sector employment, work experience, tenure, and firm size. Controlling for selection into the labor force does not have a severe impact on the coefficients of the eastern and western samples, though they do illustrate a negative selection out of the labor force except for eastern females. The coefficients presented can be interpreted as the expected percentage increase in monthly gross salary for each additional year of schooling obtained. The significance relates to the statistical significance of the difference from the 1990 base years. Cross-section calculations show that the returns to any individual year are significant, but returns are not always significantly different from one another.

Table 6

Returns to Education by Region and Gender

	Males		Females	
	West	East	West	East
Years of Education	0.079***	0.050***	0.070***	0.064***
	(0.003)	(0.003)	(0.006)	(0.004)
Years of Education*1991	–0.005	–0.003	0.005	–0.012*
	(0.004)	(0.006)	(0.008)	(0.006)
Years of Education*1992	–0.000	–0.002	–0.004	0.016**
	(0.004)	(0.006)	(0.009)	(0.008)
Years of Education*1993	0.001	0.010**	0.007	0.011
	(0.004)	(0.005)	(0.009)	(0.007)
Years of Education*1994	–0.004	0.005	0.002	0.005
	(0.004)	(0.005)	(0.008)	(0.006)
Years of Education*1995	–0.005	0.008	–0.003	0.004
	(0.004)	(0.006)	(0.008)	(0.007)
Years of Education*1996	–0.005	0.012**	0.001	0.004
	(0.004)	(0.006)	(0.008)	(0.007)
Years of Education*1997	–0.007*	0.011**	–0.002	0.003
	(0.004)	(0.006)	(0.008)	(0.007)
Years of Education*1998	–0.006	0.012**	–0.006	0.004
	(0.004)	(0.006)	(0.007)	(0.007)
Years of Education*1999	–0.003	0.017***	-0.005	0.005
	(0.004)	(0.006)	(0.007)	(0.007)
Years of Education*2000	0.005	0.024***	0.004	–0.001
	(0.004)	(0.005)	(0.007)	(0.006)
Years of Education*2001	0.008**	0.020***	0.003	0.008
	(0.003)	(0.005)	(0.007)	(0.007)
Years of Education*2002	0.005	0.021***	–0.005	0.010
	(0.004)	(0.006)	(0.007)	(0.007)
Years of Education*2003	–0.000	0.026***	–0.004	0.014**
	(0.004)	(0.006)	(0.007)	(0.007)
Years of Education*2004	0.002	0.026***	–0.000	0.018***
	(0.004)	(0.006)	(0.007)	(0.007)
Years of Education*2005	0.001	0.033***	0.007	0.014*
	(0.004)	(0.006)	(0.007)	(0.007)
Years of Education*2006	0.002	0.038***	0.010	0.022***
	(0.004)	(0.006)	(0.007)	(0.007)
Years of Education*2007	0.006*	0.033***	0.006	0.018**
	(0.004)	(0.007)	(0.007)	(0.007)
Constant	5.903***	5.283***	5.923***	4.723***
	(0.037)	(0.046)	(0.076)	(0.060)
Lambda	–0.160	-0.108	–0.0651	0.0343
	(0.009)	(0.019)	(0.009)	(0.016)
Wald test of indep. equations	300.0	49.03	78.24	2.298
Censored Obs.	11,124	6,350	36,628	12,970
Observations	44,681	21,356	49,896	23,595

Notes: Robust standard errors in parentheses, *** $p < 0.01$, ** $p < 0.05$, * $p < 0.1$. Dependent variable: log of gross monthly earnings, Additional controls: tenure (squ,), experience (squ.), public sector, firm size, year dummies.

Source: SOEP 1990 – 2007.

Western men realize returns to education of 7.9 percent in 1990, and in most of the other years returns are not statistically different. In 2007, returns rise to 8.5 percent. The returns for eastern men begin at 5.0 percent and rise quickly and statistically significantly until 2007. Eastern males achieve returns to each additional year of schooling on the same level as western males first in 2005. This can be explained as the time it takes the males to obtain new knowledge and find how to apply their own knowledge to their respective work in the free-market economy. The results are slightly different for western and eastern women. Western women begin with a rate of return of 7.0 percent for each additional year of schooling in 1990, and results are not statistically different from this rate in all of the sample years. Eastern women begin with a rate of 6.4 percent, and after a temporary decrease in 1991 this increases to over 8 percent after 2003. This means that the returns for eastern women actually exceed those of western women. This may be due to the emphasis placed on education and work in the former East Germany. Returns to education for western women are higher than those for eastern women without controlling for selection into the labor force.[4] This means more women are educated and working in the eastern states, while more women chose not to work in the western states.

5.4 Migrants

It is of interest to determine how individuals who received their human capital in the eastern states would be rewarded in the western states. In order to examine this, migrants are defined as those who grew up in the eastern states and moved to the western states after unification. The results for these individuals are presented in Table 7. The first model deals with both males and females, while the second deals with only males. The number of female migrants in the sample was too small to create a model for only females. The model contains control variables for years, hours worked, public sector employment, and firm size. According to the results for male and female migrants, tenure realizes returns of 2.5 percent (Model 1), which is above that of eastern males and females when controlling for the same variables (Table 5). Men see returns of even 3.5 percent, which is clearly above the rate of return for both westerners and easterners who did not move to the West. Total work experience is equally remunerated for migrants as for easterners who stayed in East Germany (Model 1 and Model 3). However, migrants are punished even harder for work experience they gained before unification: every year of employment in the socialist system reduces earnings by almost 2 percent.[5] In contrast, work experience from 1990 has a lower return for male workers who migrated West (Model 3) than for East German stayers. It seems that the importance of work experience for the determination of wages has been shifted towards the importance of tenure in the case of migrants.

4 These results are not shown in the table, but are available from the authors upon request.

5 This result is robust to the inclusion of age and age squared as additional control variables in the wage regression.

Table 7

Returns to Human Capital for Migrants

	All		Males	
	Model (1)	Model (2)	Model (3)	Model (4)
Years of Education	0.084*** (0.003)	0.010 (0.029)	0.082*** (0.004)	–0.014 (0.033)
Tenure	0.025*** (0.003)	0.039*** (0.003)	0.035*** (0.004)	0.043*** (0.004)
Tenure squ.	–0.001*** (0.000)	–0.001*** (0.000)	–0.001*** (0.000)	–0.001*** (0.000)
Experience		0.009*** (0.003)		0.004 (0.004)
Experience squ.		–0.001** (0.000)		–0.001* (0.000)
Experience before 1990	–0.019*** (0.003)		–0.018*** (0.004)	
Experience before 1990 squ.	0.001*** (0.000)		0.000*** (0.000)	
Experience from 1990	0.055*** (0.009)		0.036*** (0.011)	
Experience from 1990 squ.	–0.001*** (0.000)		–0.001 (0.001)	
Years of Education*1992		0.057 (0.036)		0.069* (0.038)
Years of Education*1993		0.079** (0.033)		0.092** (0.038)
Years of Education*1994		0.056* (0.032)		0.057 (0.037)
Years of Education*1995		0.061* (0.032)		0.068* (0.037)
Years of Education*1996		0.047 (0.032)		0.051 (0.037)
Years of Education*1997		0.053 (0.032)		0.066* (0.037)
Years of Education*1998		0.069** (0.032)		0.087** (0.036)
Years of Education*1999		0.074** (0.033)		0.111*** (0.038)
Years of Education*2000		0.065** (0.031)		0.093*** (0.036)
Years of Education*2001		0.074** (0.030)		0.096*** (0.035)
Years of Education*2002		0.067** (0.030)		0.084** 0.035)

Continued next page

Table 7 Continued

	All		Males	
	Model (1)	Model (2)	Model (3)	Model (4)
Years of Education*2003		0.066**		0.096***
		(0.031)		(0.035)
Years of Education*2004		0.082***		0.110***
		(0.030)		(0.036)
Years of Education*2005		0.080***		0.111***
		(0.030)		(0.035)
Years of Education*2006		0.078**		0.109***
		(0.030)		(0.036)
Years of Education*2007		0.078**		0.110***
		(0.030)		(0.035)
Lambda	–0.268	–0.239	–0.278	–0.261
	(0.064)	(0.086)	(0.061)	(0.066)
Wald test of indep. equations	38.87	20.18	26.91	23.08
Censored Obs.	1,388	1,388	266	266
Observations	3,298	3,298	1,427	1,427

Notes: Robust standard errors in parentheses, *** $p < 0.01$, ** $p < 0.05$, * $p < 0.1$. Dependent variable: log of gross monthly earnings, Additional controls: public sector, firm size, year dummies, female dummy.

Source: SOEP 1991 – 2007.

The returns to education for those migrating west have a rapid rise towards and above western levels after unification. Two years following unification, returns to education for males and females were not yet significant. However, in almost all subsequent years, returns to education were substantial and significantly higher than in the base year, 1991.[6] For males, the rate of return fluctuated between the eastern and western levels until 1998. From this time on, returns for the migrants were at or higher than western levels. This would indicate that education obtained in the eastern states was rewarded similarly to western education. It may also be due to the selection into migration, as it has been found that those with favorable characteristics, such as hard-to-observe cognitive and non-cognitive skills, were more likely to migrate west after the fall of the wall.

5.5 Returns to School Leaving Degrees

Coefficients on specific school leaving degrees for the years 1991 to 2007 are reported for males in Table 8, and in Table 9 for females. The rates of returns in each year are calculated and displayed in Figure 1. Returns to university, technical

6 This analysis is based on the years 1991 to 2007, and does not use wave 1990, since almost no East-West migrants were observed during the interviews in 1990.

college, high school (with or without an additional vocational degree) and apprenticeships are calculated separately for eastern and western males and females in reference to those with no further education following the completion of secondary or intermediate school. Though returns to each additional year of schooling have reached high levels of equality between the eastern and western states, findings show that returns to specific degrees earned in the eastern states are below western levels. Beginning with western men, returns to a university degree are steady around 60 percent, while those for a technical college degree, high school degree and apprenticeship saw increases between 1990 and 2007.[7] Returns to technical college began at approximately 20 percent, while returns to high school had a higher payoff of about 35 percent. The returns to apprenticeship were clearly lower with about 15 percent. The returns to a university degree in the eastern states were lower for men, averaging out to around 45 percent. As Figure 1 shows, between 1990 and 2007 there was a clear upward trend for the returns to a university degree in East Germany. At the same time, returns to technical college and apprenticeships began higher than western levels, but dropped significantly in the years following unification. This reflects the compressed wage structure prevalent in the German Democratic Republic.

Results for eastern and western women are slightly different. Between 1991 and 2007 the returns to a university degree for western women increased from approximately 50 percent to around 60 percent, which corresponds to the level of western males. Returns to technical college, high school, and apprenticeships also increased at roughly the same rates, and remain at lower levels than the returns to university. Conversely, returns for all educational degrees fell for eastern women who had initially higher returns to technical college, high school and apprenticeships than women in West Germany. The downward trend was somewhat weaker for university and high school degrees, but eastern women received lower rates of return to a university and high school degree than western women by 2007. Returns for technical college started at slightly under 30 percent and fell to below 20 percent. Similarly, returns for apprenticeships began at slightly below 20 percent and fell to roughly 10 percent in the years following unification. These results indicate that the returns to specific school leaving degrees are not as large in the eastern states, which is again a reflection of the remnants of a more constricted wage structure in the GDR.

---

[7] However, as is evident from Table 8 and Table 9, most of the changes in the rates of return to education were not statistically significant.

Table 8

Returns to Educational Degrees: Males

	West				East			
	Univ.	Techn. College	High School	Apprent.	Univ.	Techn. College	High School.	Apprent.
Degree	0.645***	0.237***	0.353***	0.138***	0.482***	0.301***	0.297***	0.191***
	(0.030)	(0.028)	(0.041)	(0.026)	(0.066)	(0.069)	(0.076)	(0.066)
Degree*1991	–0.070	–0.046	–0.060	–0.053	–0.025	0.032	–0.075	–0.012
	(0.043)	(0.039)	(0.057)	(0.036)	(0.110)	(0.115)	(0.136)	(0.109)
Degree*1992	–0.027	–0.045	–0.099	–0.045	0.173	0.202	0.257	0.211
	(0.043)	(0.040)	(0.061)	(0.037)	(0.297)	(0.299)	(0.311)	(0.296)
Degree*1993	–0.023	–0.034	–0.064	–0.044	–0.005	–0.061	–0.025	–0.062
	(0.042)	(0.039)	(0.055)	(0.036)	(0.089)	(0.095)	(0.118)	(0.087)
Degree*1994	–0.077*	–0.086**	–0.113**	–0.077**	–0.046	–0.091	–0.112	–0.086
	(0.043)	(0.040)	(0.054)	(0.037)	(0.130)	(0.133)	(0.150)	(0.128)
Degree*1995	–0.078*	–0.077**	–0.134**	–0.066*	–0.052	–0.081	–0.070	–0.098
	(0.042)	(0.039)	(0.058)	(0.036)	(0.138)	(0.141)	(0.158)	(0.136)
Degree*1996	–0.025	0.002	–0.044	–0.003	–0.085	–0.163*	–0.099	–0.158*
	(0.047)	(0.045)	(0.059)	(0.043)	(0.087)	(0.092)	(0.118)	(0.085)
Degree*1997	–0.083*	–0.069*	–0.141**	–0.060	–0.143*	–0.214**	–0.115	–0.206***
	(0.044)	(0.041)	(0.063)	(0.039)	(0.082)	(0.086)	(0.110)	(0.079)
Degree*1998	–0.026	0.009	–0.059	0.015	–0.118	–0.204*	–0.230	–0.193*
	(0.043)	(0.040)	(0.056)	(0.038)	(0.113)	((0.116)	(0.145)	(0.110)
Degree*1999	–0.004	0.013	–0.058	0.007	–0.243**	–0.365***	–0.217*	–0.344***
	(0.043)	(0.041)	(0.057)	(0.038)	(0.111)	(0.115)	(0.130)	(0.109)
Degree*2000	0.008	0.058	0.032	–0.003	–0.017	–0.200**	0.080	–0.129*
	(0.038)	(0.035)	(0.053)	(0.033)	(0.078)	(0.080)	(0.099)	(0.076)
Degree*2001	0.011	0.026	0.043	–0.015	0.010	–0.148*	–0.062	–0.085
	(0.038)	(0.036)	(0.054)	(0.033)	(0.081)	(0.081)	(0.103)	(0.078)
Degree*2002	0.010	0.058	0.056	–0.006	0.008	–0.148*	–0.078	–0.090
	(0.041)	(0.039)	(0.055)	(0.037)	(0.088)	(0.089)	(0.130)	(0.086)
Degree*2003	–0.062	–0.001	–0.047	–0.040	–0.018	–0.225**	–0.103	–0.166*
	(0.041)	(0.039)	(0.057)	(0.036)	(0.091)	(0.092)	(0.131)	(0.088)
Degree*2004	–0.010	0.052	0.020	0.009	–0.007	–0.218**	–0.027	–0.151*
	(0.044)	(0.042)	(0.059)	(0.039)	(0.093)	(0.093)	(0.116)	(0.090)
Degree*2005	–0.037	0.023	–0.021	–0.024	–0.022	–0.279**	–0.169	–0.206*
	(0.043)	(0.041)	(0.059)	(0.039)	(0.108)	(0.109)	(0.147)	(0.106)
Degree*2006	–0.021	0.051	0.022	–0.010	0.122	–0.109	–0.058	–0.121
	(0.045)	(0.043)	(0.064)	(0.041)	(0.103)	(0.104)	(0.130)	(0.100)
Degree*2007	–0.002	0.022	–0.028	–0.013	0.119	–0.106	–0.067	–0.060
	(0.045)	(0.044)	(0.059)	(0.041)	(0.100)	(0.101)	(0.126)	(0.098)
Lambda	–0.159				–0.110			
	(0.011)				(0.017)			
Wald test	254.4				40.63			
Cens. Obs.	19,770				8,207			
Obs.	63,328				23,213			

Notes: Dependent variable: log of gross monthly earnings, Additional controls: tenure (squ,), experience (squ.), public sector, firm size, year dummies.

Source: SOEP 1990 – 2007.

Table 9

Returns to Educational Degrees: Females

	West				East			
	Univ.	Techn. College	High School	Apprent.	Univ.	Techn. College	High School.	Apprent.
Degree	0.552***	0.226***	0.295***	0.177***	0.464***	0.284***	0.328***	0.181***
	(0.052)	(0.040)	(0.067)	(0.037)	(0.039)	(0.057)	(0.067)	(0.039)
Degree*1991	0.018	0.016	0.065	–0.000	–0.051	0.043	0.031	0.028
	(0.078)	(0.058)	(0.090)	(0.054)	(0.091)	(0.112)	(0.134)	(0.090)
Degree*1992	–0.056	–0.035	–0.013	–0.030	0.345**	0.364**	0.393*	0.340**
	(0.081)	(0.058)	(0.095)	(0.055)	(0.167)	(0.177)	(0.201)	(0.167)
Degree*1993	0.014	–0.018	0.086	–0.011	0.005	–0.060	–0.005	–0.040
	(0.079)	(0.062)	(0.094)	(0.058)	(0.104)	(0.126)	(0.156)	(0.104)
Degree*1994	–0.023	–0.050	0.007	–0.052	0.127	0.002	0.160	0.114
	(0.076)	(0.056)	(0.085)	(0.052)	(0.080)	(0.122)	(0.136)	(0.080)
Degree*1995	–0.074	–0.022	0.026	–0.036	0.067	0.004	0.091	0.052
	(0.075)	(0.056)	(0.087)	(0.054)	(0.095)	(0.116)	(0.160)	(0.096)
Degree*1996	–0.008	0.006	0.018	–0.035	0.045	0.032	0.175	0.040
	(0.073)	(0.057)	(0.093)	(0.056)	(0.091)	(0.115)	(0.165)	(0.091)
Degree*1997	–0.032	–0.027	0.017	–0.051	0.043	0.032	0.112	0.049
	(0.071)	(0.056)	(0.092)	(0.055)	(0.087)	(0.109)	(0.186)	(0.087)
Degree*1998	–0.062	–0.003	–0.038	–0.029	0.131	0.148	0.243*	0.147
	(0.069)	(0.056)	(0.092)	(0.054)	(0.098)	(0.111)	(0.147)	(0.098)
Degree*1999	–0.068	–0.042	–0.021	–0.064	0.157	0.159	0.329**	0.185*
	(0.068)	(0.055)	(0.091)	(0.053)	(0.105)	(0.117)	(0.142)	(0.104)
Degree*2000	0.024	0.050	0.133	0.027	–0.059	–0.088	–0.033	–0.062
	(0.063)	(0.053)	(0.082)	(0.050)	(0.070)	(0.082)	(0.125)	(0.071)
Degree*2001	0.023	0.010	0.175**	0.017	–0.060	–0.156**	0.077	–0.102*
	(0.063)	(0.053)	(0.082)	(0.050)	(0.060)	(0.075)	(0.113)	(0.061)
Degree*2002	–0.020	0.053	0.194**	0.052	–0.104	–0.173**	–0.043	–0.178**
	(0.067)	(0.055)	(0.085)	(0.052)	(0.074)	(0.086)	(0.124)	(0.074)
Degree*2003	–0.042	0.001	0.120	0.040	–0.041	–0.132	0.129	–0.143*
	(0.074)	(0.058)	(0.085)	(0.056)	(0.070)	(0.082)	(0.123)	(0.075)
Degree*2004	0.002	0.029	0.062	0.021	0.029	–0.084	0.084	–0.056
	(0.068)	(0.057)	(0.093)	(0.055)	(0.090)	(0.100)	(0.137)	(0.091)
Degree*2005	0.032	–0.005	0.133	0.043	–0.002	–0.093	0.076	–0.089
	(0.072)	(0.062)	(0.087)	(0.060)	(0.076)	(0.089)	(0.130)	(0.078)
Degree*2006	0.116	0.124**	0.140	0.086	0.025	–0.109	0.013	–0.086
	(0.071)	(0.060)	(0.086)	(0.058)	(0.081)	(0.093)	(0.110)	(0.083)
Degree*2007	0.080	0.069	0.069	0.078	0.027	–0.096	–0.056	–0.066
	(0.068)	(0.058)	(0.086)	(0.056)	(0.086)	(0.097)	(0.121)	(0.086)
Lambda	–0.0872				0.0434			
	(0.009)				(0.018)			
Wald test	157.8				3.163			
Cens. Obs.	49,996				14,010			
Obs.	66,553				24,635			

Notes: Dependent variable: log of gross monthly earnings, Additional controls: tenure (squ,), experience (squ.), public sector, firm size, year dummies.

Source: SOEP 1990 – 2007.

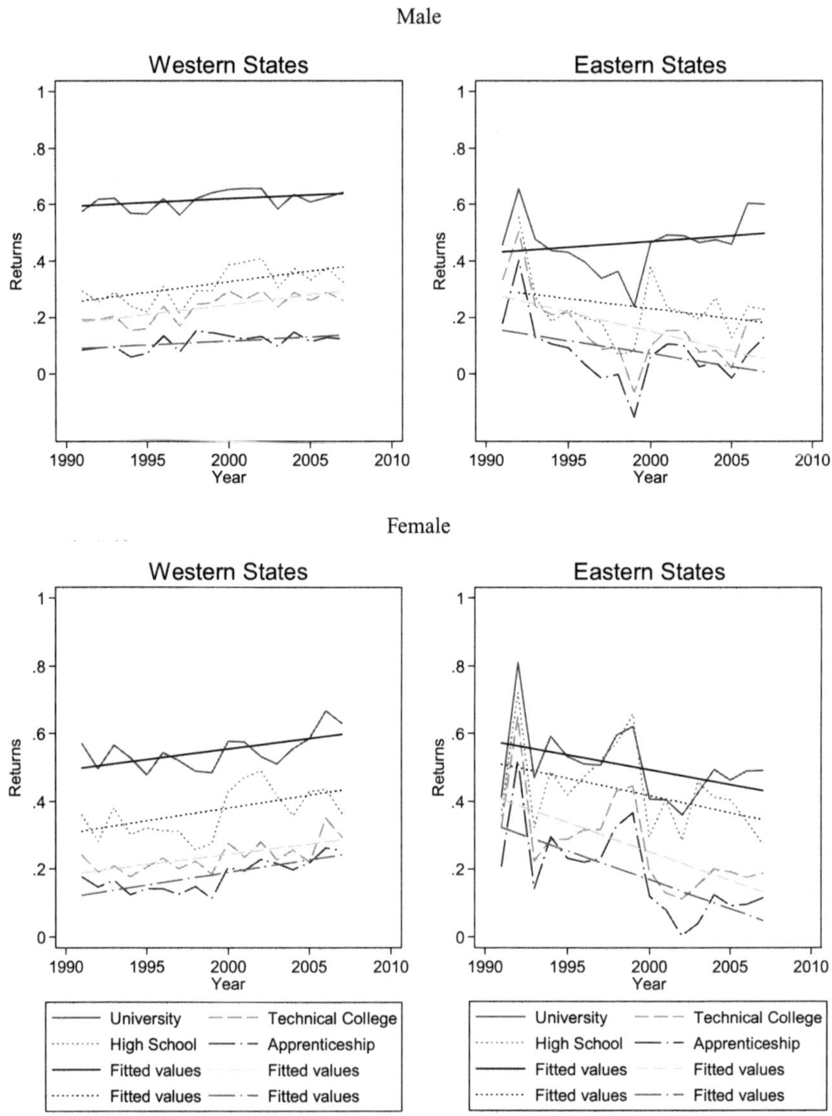

Source: SOEP Data, 1991 – 2007.

Figure 1: Returns to Educational Degrees

6. Conclusion

German unification in 1989 created a natural experiment of how human capital obtained in a socialist system would be rewarded in a free-market economy. It could be expected that under communism the returns to education would be low relative to levels in the free-market system. Upon unification, they may fall slightly in the years immediately following unification before beginning to rise to western levels. Experience obtained in the socialist system would not be expected to have high returns, as many of the skills learned in the socialist system were not of use in the free-market system. Finally, easterners migrating to the western states following unification could be examined to see how they were rewarded in the functioning western system.

Findings of the study show that returns to education for easterners did fall during the transition from the socialist economy to the free-market economy. In the years following transition, the returns to each additional year of schooling rose to western levels. What is interesting is that though the returns to each additional year of schooling are on the same level for easterners and westerners, the returns to specific degrees are higher in the western states. This signifies that the income structure is more compressed in the eastern states, in turn reducing the monetary value placed on higher degrees.

Returns to experience were also found to be lower in the eastern states, and it rose for both men and women in the post-unification years. This means that experience obtained in the German Democratic Republic was not of as high value in the western system, but that easterners were able to acquire new skills, which is shown through the rise of the returns to experience. This can also be seen in the migrant sample, as the returns to their experience over the years 1991 until 2007 averaged only about 1 percent for men and women. These levels are still short of western standard, which means the transferability of on-the-job knowledge was minimal. At the same time, the rise in the return to years of schooling for the migrants shows that much of the knowledge obtained through the formal schooling process was relevant in the free-market system.

In general, the simple OLS estimations controlling for selection into the labor force show a general convergence between the eastern and western states in the returns to human capital. Unobserved heterogeneity is not controlled for in the model, and it would be useful to repeat the estimations using different models. Furthermore, the returns to human capital rose more rapidly for women than for men. It may be useful to examine individual sectors to look more closely at where the inequalities lie.

References

Ammermüller, A. / *Weber,* A. M. (2005): Educational Attainment and Returns to Education in Germany : An Analysis by Subject of Degree, Gender and Region, ZEW Discussion Papers, 2907, ZEW – Zentrum für Europäische Wirtschaftsforschung / Center for European Economic Research.

Becker, G. S. (1964): Human Capital: A Theoretical and Empirical Analysis, with Special Reference to Education. New York: National Bureau of Economic Research.

Bird, E. J. / *Schwarze,*J. / *Wagner,* G. G. (1994): "Wage Effects of the Move toward Free Markets in East-Germany," Industrial & Labor Relations Review, 47, 390 – 400.

Chase, R. S. (1997): Markets for Communist Human Capital: Returns to Education and Experience in the Czech Republic and Slovakia, Working Papers, 770, Economic Growth Center, Yale University.

Gang, I. N. / *Yun,* M.-S. (2003): "Decomposing Male Inequality Change in East Germany During Transition," Schmollers Jahrbuch (Proceedings of the "5th International Conference of German Socio-Economic Panel Study Users", ed. by Elke Holst, Jennifer Hunt, and Jürgen Schupp), 123, 43 – 53.

Haisken-Denew, J. P., / *Frick,* J. R. (2005): Desktop Companion to the German Socio-Economic Panel Study (GSOEP), Version 8.0 – Dec 2005, Updated to Wave 21 (U), DIW Berlin, Berlin.

Heckman, J. J. (1979): "Sample Selection Bias as a Specification Error," Econometrica, 47, 153 – 161.

Krueger, A. B. / *Pischke,* J.-S. (1992): A Comparative Analysis of East and West German Labor Markets: Before and After Unification, National Bureau of Economic Research Working Paper, 4154, National Bureau of Economic Research.

Mincer, J. (1974): Schooling, Experience and Earnings. New York: Columbia University Press.

Münich, D. / *Svejnar,* J. / *Terrell,* K. (2005): "Returns to Human Capital under the Communist Wage Grid and During the Transition to a Market Economy," The Review of Economics and Statistics, 87, 100 – 123.

Orazem, P. F. / *Vodopivec,* M. (1995): "Winners and Losers in Transition: Returns to Education, Experience, and Gender in Slovenia," World Bank Economic Review, 9, 201 – 230.

Schwarze, J. (1991a): "Ausbildung und Einkommen von Männern," Mitteilungen aus der Arbeitsmarkt- und Berufsforschung (MittAB), 24, 63 – 69.

– (1991b): "Einkommensverläufe in der DDR von 1989 bis 1990 – Unbeobachtete Heterogenität und erste Auswirkungen der marktwirtschaftlichen Orientierung," in Lebenslagen im Wandel – Zur Einkommensdynamik in Deutschland seit 1984, ed. by U. Rendtel and G. Wagner. Frankfurt am Main / New York: Campus, 188 – 212.

Wagner, G. G. / *Frick,* J. R. / *Schupp,* J. (2007): "The German Socio-Economic Panel Study – Scope, Evolution and Enhancements," Schmollers Jahrbuch, 127.

Returns to Human Capital in Germany Post-Unification

Comment

By Wolfgang Scheremet*

In their study, Lupo and Anger investigate returns to human capital among employees in East Germany following reunification. This line of inquiry is relevant for economic policy, irrespective of the specific object of investigation. International and intertemporal structural change necessitates that employees permanently adapt their human capital in order to remain employed and secure high wages. This is particularly relevant with regard to East Germany, where years of pent-up structural change took place suddenly, in an extremely compressed timeframe. The innovative element of this study is its estimation of returns to human capital over time. The study shows that education pays off, even in times of profound structural transformation. According to the results of Lupo and Anger's panel study, human capital returns in East Germany reached near parity with the West in a relatively short timeframe. If one takes into account that highly qualified employees have a much lower risk of being unemployed, the total returns provided by educational investments are even higher.

The data used in the study – including endogenous gross monthly wages from employment, as well as exogenous variables, such as general work experience and tenure at a given firm – are marked by significant structural change. The number of employees in East Germany fell by approximately one-third between 1989 and 1992 (see Figure 1a). Women, older individuals and those with fewer qualifications were particularly hard hit by job losses.[1] Despite rising unemployment, average income over this period in the East nearly doubled. While the average East German employee earned just 36% of his counterpart in the West in 1989, this figure rose to 63% by 1992. Wages in the East continued to gain rapidly on the West through 1995, when the East-West wage relation stood at just under 75%. Between 1996 and 2008, however, additional gains on the West were marginal; the wage relation was 78% in 2008 (see Figure 1b).

---

* Federal Ministry of Economics and Technology (BMWi), Scharnhorststr. 34–37, 11019 Berlin. E-mail: wolfgang.scheremet@bmwi.bund.de.

1 cf. Jennifer Hunt, Determinants of Non-Employment and Unemployment duration in East Germany, NBER Working Paper Series – Working Paper 7128, 1999.

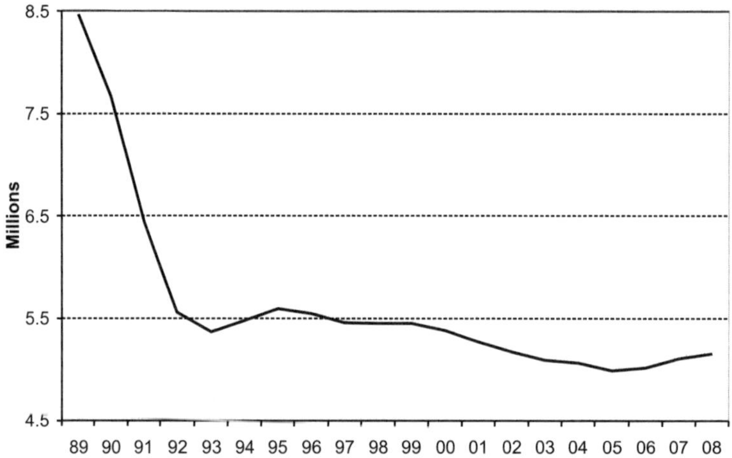

(a) Employees – East German states, excluding Berlin

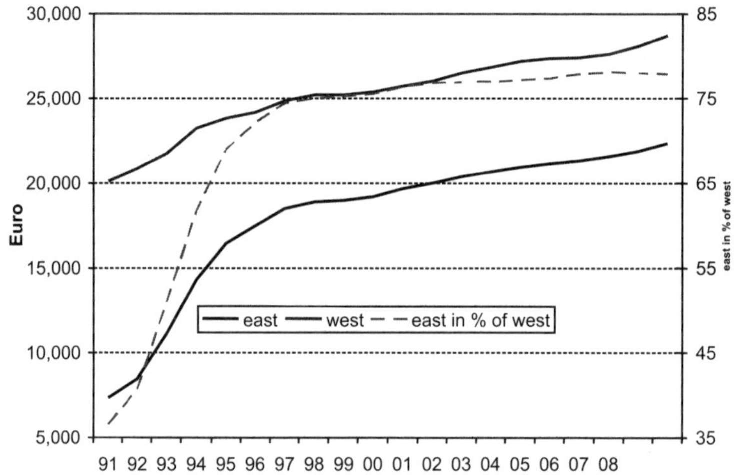

(b) Gross wages per employee

Source: DIW, NAS for East Germany; Arbeitskreis "Volkswirtschaftliche Gesamtrechnungen der Länder," series 1, volume 2.

Figure 1

Data

Lupo and Anger look exclusively at full-time wage employees, excluding the self-employed from their analysis. This approach is justified under consideration of the data source, as income data collected in surveys from the self-employed are less reliable. The filtering of the data in this manner does somewhat limit the study's ability to account for absolute human capital returns, however. On average, the self-employed (in non-agricultural sectors) have higher incomes.[2] They are also more qualified and have spent longer in school (e.g. studying to become lawyers, doctors, accountants or architects – the traditional liberal professions). The comparison between East and West Germany is less skewed by this data omission towards the end of the surveyed period, as the share of population indicating they were self-employed was only half as high in the East immediately after reunification (East: 5.1% vs. West: 10%), but has been on par with the West since 2005 (around 11%).

Lupo and Anger base their estimates on gross monthly wages. As gross monthly wages also depend on actual hours worked (which can vary between individuals), the authors control – correctly – for hours worked in their calculations. Estimates based on hourly wages would also have been possible, as the data pool contains information on working hours.

Years of education, general work experience, and tenure with a given firm are used as indicators of human capital. It is highly unlikely that these variables are fully independent of one another, however. There is a positive relationship between an individual's qualifications and the likelihood that he or she is employed. We can therefore expect additional qualifications (years in school) to be associated with shorter periods of unemployment and greater work experience. We can assume this has impacted the results.

Due to a lack of data, the costs and opportunity costs of additional years of schooling were not taken into account in the calculation of returns to education. If an individual enrolls in university instead of entering a trainee program, for example, the opportunity cost of the income forfeited due to a longer period of education must be taken into account when calculating returns to education.

Results

Transition Years

Lupo and Anger explain the decline in returns to human capital in West Germany in the early transition years (Tables 2 and 3) in terms of the large influx of workers from the East. The labor market in West Germany was nevertheless extremely robust in 1989–1991. Job creation was strong and the employment rate declined significantly. Labor market demand was strong enough to absorb the flood of migrants from the East. This understanding of the West German labor market is not contradicted by Lupo and Anger's data when one conducts a close inspection

---

2 In SOEP Wave P (1999), full-time employees grossed on average 2,474 euros / month; the self-employed, by contrast, earned 2,647 euros. *Source:* Dierk Hirschel and Joachim Merz, Was erklärt hohe Arbeitseinkommen der Selbständigen? Eine Mikroanalyse mit Daten des Sozio-ökonomischen Panels, MPRA Paper No. 5976, 2007.

of the coefficients as well as the standard error in Tables 2 and 3 of Lupo and Anger's study. The coefficients in the calculations for West Germany do decline slightly, yet in contrast to East Germany, it is unlikely that the coefficients in each individual year for West Germany diverge significantly (for women and men). A formal test for significant divergence in the coefficients for West German employees for the years 1989, 1990, and 1991 would help to bolster the study's argument.

The decline in individual returns to educational investment in East Germany in the early transition years is less surprising: Following reunification, the labor market in East Germany underwent a period of dramatic structural change and was characterized by unstable employment biographies (see Figure 1a). Wages were also unstable, and the impacts exerted by factors such as education and work experience were less pronounced. This is also evident in the decline of the adjusted R-square value.

Returns to Education and Experience over Time

Lupo and Anger calculate returns to human capital (i.e. years of schooling, general work experience as well as tenure within a given firm) in East and West Germany over time (Tables 4 and 6). Returns to experience in East Germany were not significantly divergent from zero prior to 2004. Only over the last five years have they rapidly approached levels in the West. While returns to experience for women were much higher than they were for men, they were also subject to greater fluctuations. Despite the gains made on the West, returns to education for both sexes remained lower in the East. The strong fluctuations and lower significance in the first ten years following reunification are likely attributable to the large structural changes underway in the economy as well as the unstable employment biographies of the East German populace.

The trend is somewhat different in the case of returns to education. Here, returns in the West were also for the most part constant. In contrast to returns to experience, however, returns to education for women in East Germany were not significantly below that for West German women. From 2003 onward, however, returns to education for women in East Germany rose significantly. In the early 1990s, returns to education for East German men were considerably below that for West German men. From 1993 onward, returns for East German men also rose quickly, reaching parity with the West in 2005.

Lupo and Anger account for this process of "catching up" with the assertion that human capital acquired under the communist system produced lower returns. The authors contend that as East German employees gradually acquired new human capital under the free-market system, returns to education in the East progressively rose to the level of the West. This is a plausible explanation. The data might also be explained in terms of the total collapse of the labor market in East Germany in the years immediately following reunification, however. From this perspective, higher returns for East German employees are a function of the normalization of the labor market at the end of the 1990s. The labor market in the early transition years was not only characterized by unstable employment biographies (as reflected in the high variance of the dependent variables); the institutions that govern wage formation also played a much less prominent role in East Germany. Furthermore, while West German wage scales – for example, with regard to compensation for formal qualifications – were quickly adopted in the East, the East German collective bargaining landscape was highly fragmented and a much lower percentage of workers in the East were paid under collective wage agreements. In such an environment, variables such as education and work experience that are normally relevant for compensation play a relatively smaller role. In this way, the standard explanation offered for rising human capital returns in the East may have only had a determining effect following the normalization of the labor market in the late 1990s.

Returns to School Leaving Degrees over Time

The trends exhibited by the data on returns to school leaving degrees are somewhat surprising. While returns to education and experience rose over time for male and female East German employees across all degrees, the trend for returns to school leaving degrees is downward at most degree levels, particularly for women. Only men with a university degree displayed constant returns over time (see Figure 1, Lupo & Anger). Nevertheless, for all degree levels there was a structural break in 1999 / 2000. A stable trend over the entire surveyed period was not observed. There is a need for additional analysis in this area.

Participants

Wolf Amster-Blankenfeld	Bundesministerium der Finanzen
Siegfried Angelus	Bundesministerium für Wirtschaft und Technologie
Silke Anger	DIW Berlin
Thomas K. Bauer	RWI Essen
Heike Belitz	DIW Berlin
Ansgar Belke	DIW Berlin
Ulrich Blum	IWH Halle
Sebastian Böhm	Humboldt-Universität zu Berlin
Franziska Bremus	DIW Berlin
Karl Brenke	DIW Berlin
Rolf Bürkl	GfK
Herbert S. Buscher	IWH
Martin T. Clemens	IZA Bonn
Hermann Clement	
Claudio De Luca	Capital / Financial Times Deutschland
Markus Demary	Institut der deutschen Wirtschaft Köln
Arno Diekmann	Bundesministerium der Finanzen
Berend Diekmann	Bundesministerium für Wirtschaft und Technologie
Carsten Dippel	Bundesministerium für Wirtschaft und Technologie
Rupert Dörfler	Bundeskanzleramt
Ulrich Domain	Bundesministerium der Finanzen
Klaus Dornbusch	Bundesministerium für Bildung und Forschung
Alexander Eickelpasch	DIW Berlin
Michael Eilfort	Stiftung Marktwirtschaft
Heinz Engelstädter	Forschungsinstitut der IWVWW
Angela Fiedler	DIW Berlin
Dirk Fornahl	BAW Institut für regionale Wirtschaftsforschung GmbH, Bremen
Frank Fossen	DIW Berlin
Sabine Freye	IWH Halle

Joachim Frick	DIW Berlin
Christian Geinitz	Frankfurter Allgemeine Zeitung
Thomas Gerhardt	Bundesministerium der Finanzen
Johannes Geyer	DIW Berlin
Giessler	Deutsche Welle
Maren Gören	BMI
Jutta Günther	Institut für Wirtschaftsforschung Halle
Alfred Gutzler	DIW Berlin
Wolfgang Helmstädter	Bundesministerium für Verkehr, Bau und Stadtentwicklung
Gabriele Hermani	Bundesministerium des Innern
Michael Herrscher	Büro Jan Mücke, MdB
Martin Hillebrand	DIW Berlin
Norbert Hoekstra	Bundesministerium der Finanzen
Reinhard Hujer	DIW Berlin
Bettina Jahn-Thielicke	Bundesministerium für Wirtschaft und Technologie
Gunnar John	Bundesministerium der Finanzen
Tobias Kaiser	Die Welt / Berliner Morgenpost
Tomasz Kalinowski	Botschaft der Republik Polen
Rolf Ketzler	DIW Berlin
Thomas Köhler	Bundeskanzleramt
Ernst Kranz	MdB
Thomas Krause	Deutscher Bundestag
Stefan Krenz	ifo Institut, München
Ines Krug	Bundesministerium für Wirtschaft und Technologie
Annegret Künzel	Fraktion DIE LINKE
Andreas Lämmel	Mitglied des Bundestags
Harald Lehmann	Bundesverband der deutschen Volks- und Raiffeisenbanken
Michael Leisinger	Bundesministerium der Finanzen
Silke Leßenich	Bundesministerium für Verkehr, Bau und Stadtentwicklung
Georg Licht	ZEW Mannheim
Astrid Lübke	Bundesministerium der Finanzen
Axel Lubinski	Bundesministerium für Verkehr, Bau und Stadtentwicklung
Susanne Marcus	DIW Berlin
Hilary McGeachy	Australische Botschaft
Marco Mendorf	Initiative Neue Soziale Marktwirtschaft

Ralf Messer	ARGE
Carel Mohn	DIW Berlin
Nikolaus Müllershausen	Bundesministerium für Verkehr, Bau und Stadtentwicklung
Wolfgang Nagl	ifo Institut, München
Olga Nottmeyer	DIW Berlin
Regine Pankuweit	Australische Botschaft
Franz-Josef Pröpper	Pricewaterhouse Coopers
Joachim Ragnitz	ifo Institut, München
Utz-Peter Reich	
Lutz Reimers	Bundesministerium für Wirtschaft und Technologie
Eva Reinowski	IWH
Hans-Joachim Ritell	BMI
Bernd Röder	dpa
Klaus-Heiner Röhl	Institut der deutschen Wirtschaft Köln
Steffen Roth	IWP Köln
Wolfgang Schäuble	Bundesminister des Innern
Ulrich Schasse	Niedersächsisches Institut für Wirtschaftsforschung
Klaus-Werner Schatz	Freie Universität Berlin
Hartmut Schauerte	Bundesministerium für Wirtschaft und Technologie
Wolfgang Scheremet	Bundesministerium für Wirtschaft und Technologie
Sibylle Schmerbach	Humboldt-Universität zu Berlin
Hilmar Schneider	IZA Bonn
Jürgen Schupp	DIW Berlin
Dennis Snower	Institut für Weltwirtschaft in Kiel
Eugen Spitznagelx	*Institut für Arbeitsmarkt- und Berufsforschung*
Marco Sunderx	*IWH*
Trocka, Dirk	IWH
Anke Tuljus	Bundesministerium der Finanzen
Harald Uhlig	University of Chicago
Bernard Veltrup	Bundesministerium für Wirtschaft und Technologie
Michael Vöhring	Bundesministerium der Finanzen
Andreas Wessel-Terharn	Bundesministerium für Verkehr, Bau und Stadtentwicklung
Klaus F. Zimmermann	DIW Berlin
Florian Zinsmeister	DIW Berlin